WHAT YOU NEED TO KNOW
before you start your home construction project

How to Avoid the Headaches of Construction

Edwin A. Penick

Nothing in this book constitutes professional legal advice. All examples are meant only for informational purposes only. Every state has different laws and regulations related to construction practices. Therefore, you should consult an attorney or the regulation in your state before making any decision related to contracts or the construction process.

© 2019 by Edwin A. Penick

All rights reserved. Copyright under Berne Copyright Convention, Universal Copyright Convention, and Pan-American Copyright Convention. No part of this book may be reproduced, stored in a retrieval system, or transmitted in any form, or by any means, electronic, mechanical, photocopying, recording or otherwise, without prior permission of the author.

ISBN 978-0-578-57584-1
ISBN 978-0-578-58664-9 (eBook)

DEDICATION

I would like to thank the many people: my family, friends, co-workers, mentors, subcontractors, and clients who have been part of my journey so far.

TABLE OF CONTENTS

Preface
What are you building? 1
New construction 2
Renovation 2
Getting ready 4
Architectural plans and drawings 5
Specifications (selecting your finishes) 8
Allowances 10
Choosing a General Contractor... 11
Bidding 13
Proposals 14
Contracts 17
Alternate pricing 20
Change orders 21
Insurance 22
Permits 22
Inspectors and Inspections 23
Hopping on the roller coaster: starting your project 24
Life on the roller coaster: a general outline of the construction process 25
Moving in…not quite yet 26
The punch list (or, the final hurdle to Salvation) 27
Liens and lien waivers 27
Afterword 27
Appendix 28
A) Floor plan 29
B) Elevation 30
C) Wall section 31
D) Wall section detail 32
E) Specifications example 33
F) Selection sheet example 34
G) "Black hole" contract example 35
H) Short form owner-contractor agreement example 36
I) Comprehensive contract example 39
J) Change order example 54
K) Certificate of Insurance example 55
L) Drywall finishing guide 56
M) Punch List 57
N) Lien waiver 58
Glossary 59
Notes 63

PREFACE

I became a contractor for the love of building, the creative process, and helping people achieve their visions of the places they want to live. A renovation project requires daily, sometimes hourly, problem-solving. No two projects are ever the same; each presents novel and different situations and problems.

I worked as a general contractor for ten years in three different states. By some standards it was not a long time in the business, but it was long enough to learn the ins and outs of construction and put more than a few gray hairs on my head. Prior to starting my construction business, I had never worked a construction job in my life. My sole construction experience was restoring and adding two additions to a 1920s colonial-style house—my own—over the course of nine years while working a full time job.

After selling that house I decided to take the proceeds and buy and flip another house, all while still working full-time as a museum exhibition designer. Eventually the seed money from these two projects allowed me to start my construction business. My initial goal was to "flip" houses (mind you, this was a decade before "Flip or Flop" became a TV hit). I did most of the work myself, hiring subcontractors for plumbing, electrical, and drywall as most construction companies do. Over time I found it was more efficient for me to do less of the physical labor and more of the management, hiring subcontractors who were better than I was at doing the construction work.

At around the same time, people who had seen my "flip" work began to ask if I was interested in doing smaller projects on their houses. For a time I resisted. I enjoyed the freedom of working for myself on property my company owned, and the power that gave me to set my own schedules and make my own decisions. I knew that working with a client would involve a constant process of acting as an interpreter, translating the foreign language of construction work into terms they could understand, knowing that it is important to manage expectations and shoulder blame where appropriate. I also knew that working for others would put me and my business at greater risk in some ways. Certainly, the business of less than full-scale home renovation depends largely on word of mouth and positive recommendations. When there are dreams and money involved, people's emotions understandably run high. One bad experience can be ruinous for all involved. Among the clients with whom I worked best, I consistently found that, above all, they appreciated my honesty. Often clients had an idea which their budget, their timeline, or the particular characteristics of their property made difficult or impossible to achieve. (Some clients, of course, will try to ignore advice—often by changing general contractors until they find someone who will tell them what they want to hear.) Explanation is key. In construction there are laws of cause and effect. What might, to a client, seem like a minor change to a project may in fact call for serious revisions and changes in scope.

I finally got out of the business when it started to feel like I was spending more time with my lawyer than renovating homes. My aim in writing this book is to help you avoid that fate. Let's face it: general contractors do not enjoy an exemplary reputation in our society. The construction business can be a somewhat shady field with a wide range of colorful characters. I found out quickly that many chose the profession for the wrong reasons, yet were – inexplicably - given new business all the time. Comparisons to the Wild West are not that far from the truth. However, I also learned that the industry is full of good, decent people as well. It's just a question of going about finding them. This is one of the questions that needs to be answered. If you are reading this book, you are likely aware of the risks but understand, as I did, that home renovation can be a rewarding endeavor.

WHAT ARE YOU BUILDING?

The first question you need to ask before embarking on a homebuilding project is simple: what am I trying to achieve? Completion of an entirely new house? A smaller renovation of an existing element of your property, such as a deck, bathroom, or kitchen? An addition to a property? Or some combination of these?

There are practical as well as philosophical questions to consider in determining the scope of the project. The first philosophical question is: How do you live? The new construction or renovation should be designed with regard to how you live or how you want to interact with the space. Every homeowner needs a somewhat different kind of space in order to function naturally and comfortably in their home, but too often homebuilders build dwellings to correspond to an average idea of what a homebuyer would want. Trends that seem inexplicable today (faux-wood paneling, carports) seemed desirable a generation ago. Today's trends (open-concept kitchens) might seem the same way to our children. It is important to assess your own wants and needs independent of these ephemeral things. The Environmental Protection Agency has claimed the average person spends 87 percent of their lives indoors—you will spend a large portion of your life in the space you are creating. Moreover, few people desire to live through more than one or two home construction efforts in their lives—it's important to get it right the first time!

Second, it is important to ask what are your essential priorities? This is a more practical question than the one above. Do you have children? Are you planning on having more? What kinds of spaces will they need? Do you often work at home, or want no incentive to do any work at home at all? Where should the laundry room be? How about a place to watch movies? *Prioritizing,* to answer these questions is imperative. Few of us will embark on a renovation with unlimited funds. Knowing what are the key changes you wish for a renovation to achieve with your money is essential.

Now make a **master plan**! List every project that you want to do in the renovation, keeping price and priority in mind. This will allow you to sequence your project effectively and economically before design work has begun.

> My mother designed a beach house for our family when I was about 14 years old. This was a major expense for them and they had to take out a second mortgage on our home to finance the construction. She carefully thought out and drew the floor plan. The house has a wide covered wrap-around porch on three sides and eighteen windows. The bedrooms are small and the bathrooms are adequate but not luxurious by any means. The main room consists of the kitchen, dining, and living rooms combined. In all, the design reflects her conclusion that a beach house properly used does not involve spending much time inside. There is even a small outdoor shower that my brother-in-law built with hot water. Perhaps unwittingly, my mother was engaging in "design thinking"—taking into consideration how the space should be used and elaborating a design that fit those considerations. Though the house is very simple, it is still one of the most comfortable houses I have ever lived in.

While you ponder these questions may I suggest that it is prudent to live in a house for at least a year before any renovations are done. Of course, there are exceptions, such as if the property you purchased were uninhabitable or if this is not your first time renovating a home. For most, however, living in a pre-renovation home will allow you time to understand how you do and do not function within the existing structure, and to put together a master plan reflecting that lived experience.

NEW CONSTRUCTION

One of the first principles you will learn upon embarking on new home construction is that a lot of the design is out of your or your architect's control. The shape and size of the lot will start to dictate the floor plan, and depending on where you live local zoning regulations and building codes might dictate everything from the setback* (i.e. the distance from the street to the dwelling), the height, the Floor Area Ratio* (i.e. dwelling square footage to lot square footage), and even the exterior color and design.

That said, unusual lot shapes and elevations can provide an opportunity to think outside the box and create a home that is quite unique and special, if you plan well and situate your house so as to maximize lot coverage.* You could start by building a smaller structure that would allow you to add on in the future. (The planners of great subway systems used this technique to great advantage by building "stub-end" tracks pointing in the direction of future stations.) This is easily done with a carefully thought out master plan that includes design features facilitating future additions.

Examples:

1) Installing a larger electrical service panel* to allow for the addition of electrical.
2) Installing plumbing pipes in an easily accessible place.
3) Making sure that your foundation could carry a second floor addition.
4) Putting structural beams sufficient to bear the weight of a future addition in place during phase 1.

RENOVATION

Typically, renovation will involve several smaller projects you might have in mind and plan to execute over a long period of time. In this case, proper sequencing is very important and will save money and aggravation. Here are two examples of good sequencing:

1) You want to remodel your kitchen and an upstairs bathroom that happens to be above the kitchen. However, you have determined that the kitchen is your first priority. Now, a problem presents itself: work on the bathroom will almost certainly involve digging into the floor—that is, your brand new kitchen ceiling! In this case, it is better to determine first just how important the bathroom renovation is to you. It should either be performed before the kitchen renovation, or in unison with the kitchen or not at all.

2) You have a two-story house with a basement. The electrical panel is in the basement. You want to put a master suite on the second floor but you are going to renovate the bathroom on the first floor first. In this case, it would be smart to relocate electrical wire and maybe some plumbing from the basement to the second floor while you have the bathroom under construction, to prepare for the future renovation of the second-floor bedroom.

* Words or phrases with an asterisk are found in the glossary.

As you consider and plan your building project I suggest that you consider *energy efficiency* and *sustainable materials* too. I will briefly touch on each of them. However, these subjects are books unto themselves. *Energy efficiency* will cost you a bit more money in the short term, but in the long term it will pay for itself. (Depending on where you live, state and local financial incentives for "green" construction might even mean there is no or little short-term cost, either.) If you are renovating a house you should have an Energy Audit performed so you know exactly where your weakest energy points are located. Below are a few examples of Passive Solar Design construction practices.

- Siting the house so as to utilize the sun to heat your house in the winter.
- Larger roof overhangs (eaves) and passive ventilation to keep your house cooler in the summer; both these features also allow you to use the natural light throughout the day for free!
- Having a wider eave will keep the water further from your foundation, helping to keep water infiltration from your house too.

The house's envelope is very important to keep in heat and cooling as well as keeping them out. Remember, the house needs to breathe too. Furthermore, some areas of the country have a higher content of radon gas in the ground that you do not want to trap in your house.

- Using spray foam insulation instead of traditional BAT insulation helps to really seal your house from leakage and creates very nice sound isolation too. Including using special low expansion foam for sealing around the windows. There are different kinds of foam insulation that must be carefully selected and installed by experts.
- Double or triple pane windows
- Using light colored roofing to reflect the sun.
- Installing a tankless* or on Demand water heater is a good option so you are only heating water when you need it.

Materials. Using recycled or reclaimed, sustainable FSC* (Forest Stewardship Council) lumber and maintenance-free materials is a smart and environmentally conscious thing to do. Of course, no material on earth is 100 percent maintenance free, despite what the ad copy tells you. Nevertheless, there are interesting and innovative materials available. A few examples are as follows.

- Reclaimed building materials. There are various stores that stock salvage materials or new materials that have been discarded.
- Fiber cement board*
- Brick is one of the best materials for durability

In summary:

    1) How do you live?
    2) What are you essential priorities?
    3) Make a master plan!

GETTING READY

One of the biggest misconceptions about home construction projects is that the homeowner can sit back, relax, and watch the project be completed before their eyes. With very few exceptions, a successful, on-time construction project will require a substantial commitment from *you*, as well as, of course, a good GC* that can manage the project, the construction calendar, the subcontractors,* and your expectations.

Before I go further, let me first make clear six crucial points:

First, do not think that you can be your own GC. Many are tempted to assume the burden of being their own GC, either for cost reasons or because they think they will have greater creative independence in guiding the project. The fact is that contracting is a learned skill just like any other. Perhaps not as much is at stake to a GC as say, to an airline pilot, but in both professions people succeed only through experience. A good GC is worth every penny you pay them. To be sure, this is not the same as saying *every* GC is worth your business. Regardless, having a *good* GC is crucial to the success of your project.

Second, be prepared for the long haul. If you're like me, you have probably been dreaming of doing this construction project for years. Now that you've finally decided to commit to it, you'd like it done quickly. This attitude, though reasonable, will only lead to bad outcomes. It takes time to plan thoroughly for even the smallest project, so please prepare to be living with a renovation or construction effort for longer than you think.

> I once did a renovation for a couple who procrastinated until they were three months pregnant with their second child. I didn't think we would finish before she went into labor. Believe me it was close; she went into labor just a few days before we finished. However, they were lovely, understanding people and great clients.

Third, I assure you: If you are planning on building your dream home and it is your first house you have ever built from scratch, *you will not get it perfect!* Maybe if you have a ton of money and keep making costly changes you might get close. Even then there will still probably be small things that nag you. Not that you won't be happy with the end product—I say this, again, only to manage your expectations. If renovation or home construction was a process that could be perfectly anticipated from beginning to end, it would not have the reputation it does.

Fourth, as I wrote earlier, I do not recommend living in your house during a large renovation. The unpredictability of a construction project means that its stresses are magnified when you are living among them. Avoiding them if at all possible is essential not only to finishing the project but also to your short-term mental health. Obviously, not everyone has the financial means to live in temporary quarters over the long term. You may, however, want to consider this a core part of your renovation budget rather than an optional extra.

> Every house I have lived in since I was a child went through a renovation with me and/or my family living in it. It is no picnic, particularly when the stresses of construction are layered on top of those of normal family life. One client of mine decided that he and his family would live in the house despite our pleas for him to move his family out. Part of the

scope of this project was to blow the entire side of the house out. About a third of the way through, they changed their minds and moved out. I was sorry that the construction work made them miserable, but I guess they just had to find out for themselves.

Fifth, pardon the dust. Dust can range from simply bothersome to acutely toxic; in any event, it is an unavoidable and universal aspect of construction work. You should assume that everything you own that remains on your property will be covered in dust. You have probably realized by now that this point is a corollary to point no. 4. Perhaps you had an image in your mind of being able to close off part of the house to dust. In practice, you will never be able to avoid the dust completely.

Sixth, just because parts of a house have been recently remodeled doesn't mean that remodeling is "good." Many property owners, especially house flippers, do not want to spend the money on the "guts" of a house (meaning electrical, plumbing, HVAC*). They will do just enough cosmetic work to make it look decent for an unsuspecting buyer. I like to call this "remuddling." In short, do not assume that a recent remodel was done correctly.

Finally, I will let you in on a secret. No matter if the job is finished early, on time, or late, you will be more than ready to part ways with your GC even if it's on good terms. After three to 12 months or longer of having people in your house at 7 AM each morning, possibly 6 days a week, you just want them gone. I take no offense at this, and neither should any good GC. It comes with the job.

ARCHITECTURAL PLANS OR DRAWINGS

Even with a small construction project you will need some type of drawing(s). This might be a simple floor plan* or a more complex set of drawings including a site plan,* multiple elevations,* electrical, HVAC, plumbing, wall section,* and details.* In a home renovation or construction all drawings are always to **scale**.* In the definitions that follow I have attempted to give you an idea of some unfamiliar drawing terms you might encounter but the list is by no means exhaustive.

Scale is a ratio of relative size. A drawing in which one inch on paper represents one foot in reality would be expressed as 1:1.

Floor Plan is a scaled drawing illustrating the layout of the existing rooms and/or rooms to be built. The perspective is from above. There should be printed dimensions for the walls, widths of doors, windows and passageways, locations of fixtures, cabinets and other pertinent features. (See Appendix A)

Elevation is the view of the building from the side. Each side is drawn and labeled using the directional points on a compass (north, east, south, and west). These views give you a good idea of what the building will look like after construction. (See Appendix B)

Wall Section is as if you were to slice the building down the middle. The drawing allows you to see the relationships from the foundation to the roof. (See Appendix C)

Wall Section Detail is a drawing that shows a small detail of a larger drawing. This type of drawing is used to show a complicated junction with specific material details, specific decorative elements, finishes, or a part of the drawing that just needs a particular component enlarged for better clarity. (See Appendix D)

You can procure drawings from a variety of sources. Drawings might be provided by an architectural firm, a company that employs one or more licensed architects. The architect enters into a contract to design and provide you with finished drawings for your project. They might oversee the project management for an additional fee, depending on the type of firm.

Alternatively, your drawings might come from a design/build firm. A design-build firm involves one entity, the design-builder, entering into a single contract with the owner to provide both design and construction services. This means that they provide drawings, procure the necessary permits or have their subcontractors do so, and oversee construction. Such a firm might employ a staff including GCs, PMs,* carpenters etc.

Finally, you might choose to purchase architectural plans off of the Internet. I would not generally recommend this, as you can never be sure an Internet drawing will meet your local building codes and zoning regulations.

Which of these options best fits your needs is for you to determine. I would recommend interviewing some architects and design/build firms just as you will interview prospective contractors. First, you want to make sure that whomever you choose typically works within your price range. Even if a firm claims it can work to meet your financial needs, no one wants to be the "budget" client paid scant attention to by an otherwise high-end firm. Second, you want to make sure the architect or design/build firm is attentive to your ideas for the project and will use their expertise and experience to help you conceptualize a design rather than providing a cookie-cutter version they already have, or worse impose their personal ideas on your project. It is important at this stage not to be brow-beaten by a single firm into raising your budget. Within reason, there is nothing to prevent you from building the project you want within a reasonable range of costs.

There are five important cautionary points about drawings to which I want to bring your attention.

First, not all architects seem to have a good sense of current construction costs. I cannot tell you how many times we would bid on a job and our price, as well as those of our competitors, far exceeded the budget the client was told by an architect would be reasonable. Assuming we were awarded the project, we would then have to "value-engineer*" it down closer to the client's original budget, a process that no one enjoys. This can mean removing certain elements from the project and/or using cheaper materials. I was never happy about this as a contractor, and of course the client ended up disappointed as well. When being quoted a price from an architect, then, it may be useful to compare with other architects or even consult a contractor first.

> I remember a project where the architect had put the stairs in the wrong place on the drawings, meaning there was not enough headroom on the staircase to comply with the building code. The architect's suggestion, incredibly, was to build the design and hope we did not get caught by an inspector! What a stupid idea. We ended up moving the location of the stairs well before the final inspection. Though the architect should have borne the cost of his mistake, his firm never admitted fault.

Second, drawings are meant to serve as a *guide*. The majority of the drawings I have read are not complete or have discrepancies. It's possible your architect or builder will have 100 percent correct plans, but this is rare. A good GC bidding on your project will catch some of the errors in the bidding process and will inform you of their concerns.

> I had a brief association with an architect who I am convinced made a significant part of his living based on "unforeseen conditions" from his original drawings. This meant that when a GC would find problems the architect would send an underling to assess the issue(s), inevitably requiring expensive additional drawings and delaying the project possibly by weeks.

Third, even after plans go through the permitting process and are approved, that still does not necessarily make them buildable as drawn. Though it may not be obvious at first, the main purpose of a permit review is *not* to make sure that a specific drawing can be built in a specific place (this would require far too much work on the part of the reviewers). Rather, it's about making sure the plans meet the more general international building code or IBC.* This is why the building departments I have worked with always stamped a disclaimer on the drawings, which read: "Subject to field inspection." Don't be surprised if even the architect has put a note on the plans, too, asking the "GC to field verify." This is essentially a message that the architect will not assume responsibility for the implementation of the plans in real life. Surprisingly, this abdication of liability is widely accepted and almost unavoidable. Problems can be avoided, however, if the architect or design/build firm does good "field measurements"—that is, goes and measures the actual house. In addition, on renovation projects, if your architect, GC, and subcontractors have prior knowledge of the types of houses that were built in your area, they can apply that knowledge and possibly avoid some problems, too. However, just remember some houses are just unique.

> We were remodeling a house and the second floor Tongue and Groove (T&G) hardwood flooring was sagging heavily in some rooms. When the flooring subcontractor went to start to repair it, we discovered that the house second floor did not have a subfloor.* The existing finished floor had been laid just on the floor joists, which created a floor that was very spongy due to insufficient structural integrity. The first floor T&G, however, was on a subfloor. I always wondered if the original flooring contractor in the 1920's showed up before the carpenters had installed the subfloor, and installed the flooring not caring that it was incorrect. To this day it remains a mystery.

> We were once adding an addition to a house and had the first floor framed and the second floor walls built. The plans had the roof ridge* at the same height as the existing roof ridge. However, it was physically impossible to construct the house as drawn. Because of the side yard setback,* we could not change the pitch of the roof to align to the roof ridge. The only way to make the ridge connect at the same height would have required us to lower the ceiling height in the addition to less than 8 feet. In the end the roof ridge of the addition was higher than the original. Aesthetically, this was not the best solution, but unfortunately it was the only viable one.

Fourth, just because the plans say a particular room will be a particular size, this does not mean that the end result will *look* or *feel* that size. For some reason spaces look larger on paper (architectural plans) than they do in actuality. The framing and especially drywall installation process reduces the available space in the room to a noticeable degree.

Fifth, there are *always* hazards and uncertainties that emerge in a renovation project once the GC and crew begin to expose the frame of the house during the demolition process. No one really knows what lurks behind the walls.

> In one basement renovation project the plans called for the removal of an interior wall, which seemed straightforward. However, when the plaster was removed we exposed the main sewer pipe, which then needed to be relocated. On numerous occasions we removed the plaster from the walls only to find asbestos covered ductwork.

> On a lighter note, one time I was with my friend Jon salvaging some very large double sash windows from a house in Virginia dating to the 1800's. As we removed the interior plaster so that we could access the window frame, we noticed rags with brown stains on them stuffed into the walls. As we continued, we realized that these rags where covered with dried blood. We surmised the house had been used as a hospital during the Civil War and most likely the rags had been stuffed into the walls for insulation purposes. Then Jon found an unused 1855 railroad ticket. Not all of my stories are horror ones—unfortunately just most!

My lengthy point is that drawings are not final products. They could well have inherent flaws; even if they don't, there might be unforeseen issues that develop later in the construction process. A good GC (and a patient client) will "know what they don't know"—that is, they will *expect* to be surprised by certain roadblocks during the process, and will factor these into their budget and their schedules. In this way, the worst GC you could have is an overconfident one. The best will be honest and humble, realizing that no one embarking on a major renovation or construction project can fully anticipate every stage.

With that said, an experienced residential architect can make the building process much easier. This is particularly true in new construction. They are invaluable when electrical, plumbing and structural layouts are considered during the drawing process. It is important to plan where the plumbing pipes and duct work will be placed in order to conceal them as much as possible, insuring maximizing your physical and aesthetic space.

> There was one project in which the architect had placed so many LVLs* to support the first floor that we had to drop all of the duct work and plumbing pipes below them, which required us to build a bulkhead to conceal them. It was unfortunate because this wasted precious space and increased the framing and drywall cost.

SPECIFICATIONS (SELECTING YOUR FINISHES)

So you thought you were ready to start looking for a contractor? Not quite yet. At this stage it's imperative to start paying attention to your finishes, such as tile, cabinets, plumbing fixtures, windows, etc. if you have not done so already. Perhaps you considered these items during the drawing process, or at least looked casually at them. In any event, it can be a daunting process simply because there are so many different products on the market, but it can also be fun. You could start the bidding process and even the construction without choosing your finishes by using allowances.* I do not recommend that anyone follow this route because there are just to many variables. It is a sure way to bust a budget! The best way to get an accurate bid, stay on budget, and be able to compare bids to one another is to complete your choice of all the finishes *before* you start the bidding process and create a specification sheet.* (See Appendix E) This way, GCs are bidding with the same information and can quote more accurate prices for materials and labor than if they are working with hypothetical materials and labor. There is just less guesswork for everyone involved.

So how do you go about deciding on where to look or how to choose your finishes? There are several possibilities:

- The person making your drawings might be able to make some suggestions.
- If you like the fixtures in a friend's house, ask about those.
- You can browse products from home on the internet and put items in a shopping cart. Some company websites allow you to create an account and save your selections. In either case this can be printed out and taken to a local dealer. I do not recommend you order materials off the internet. Ultimately, you should actually look at everything in person before buying, because quality and comfort can be very different in reality than they appear in a picture. A higher price does *not* always mean better quality, especially in lighting and cabinetry.
- You can just start to browse by going to a plumbing or tile showroom, where a consultant can educate you on their products. They can start a file with your selections and give you a printout to pass on to the bidders.

A few tips when going through this process:

1) When selecting your materials, avoid anything that is back-ordered or close to being back-ordered. Just take my advice and find another product. It is better to have a product you like that arrives on time than one you love that arrives weeks or even months late, adding cost and stress to your construction project. In my experience, no manufacturer is entirely sure when their own product will be shipped from the plant, especially because most of these products are coming from overseas. You go to war with the army you have!

2) Beware of brand-name products sold through big box stores. Just because the product is a name brand, it does not mean it is the same product. Model numbers should be checked. For the most part, home construction is an industry where you get no more than you pay for. That said, there is a price point where cost does not necessarily get you better quality.

> Early in my construction career I purchased some marble from a big box store because it was cheap. Almost immediately after installing the material, the finish started to wear off. Thank goodness that was in my own house and not a client's.

3) There is usually no guarantee for products purchased off the internet that the material will arrive in good condition. Cracks or missing parts are commonplace, but quality control is getting better, hence my caution about using the internet for anything more than research.

4) Many showrooms are just middlemen that do not stock all their showroom samples such as tile, porcelain, or stone. Unfortunately this can introduce some uncertainty into the ordering process, as they may order the material only after they have your deposit (or, even worse, only after they have interest from enough customers to place an order). In such cases, you should ask the showroom to call the distributor with you present and verify that the distributor has the material in stock. Better yet, if your GC

is competent ask them to do this for you. In general, you will not be penalized for ordering your finishes too early; most showrooms will hold the material in their warehouse for a reasonable period of time. (However, it could get sold to someone else—it's been known to happen.)

A special note on **natural stone:** *when they say this material has "variations in color" they really mean it. What you see in the store or showroom is not what you might get—in fact, the showroom example was probably chosen for its exceptional appearance. You should expect differences in color and striation in the material you actually purchase.*

If this is all starting to feel a little overwhelming, you will appreciate my final suggestion: have your GC do the purchasing of materials for your project. Apart from saving you grief, this will also shift the responsibility to your GC to make sure that the materials are onsite on time. In addition, your GC's company should provide a warranty on the materials since they supplied them. I never gave a warranty on materials supplied by the owner (SBO*) because I had no control over their quality. There are exceptions, of course. For smaller items, it is fine to do the purchasing yourself and have your GC install them for you (OPCI*). Towel bars, toilet paper holders, drawer pulls and knobs, surface-mounted light fixtures, and ceiling fans all fall into this category.

ALLOWANCES

I do not recommend anyone use allowances because there are just too many variables; especially if you are on a strict budget, this is a sure way of going over. If you choose to use allowances for any of your finishes that *have not* been chosen at least try to get an idea beforehand what certain items might cost so as to allow you to set an appropriate dollar amount. The process is tricky simply because there is such a wide price range for such products. Two examples:

- Toilets can cost anywhere from $120 to $6,000, not including installation costs. A more expensive complicated model may also lead to more expensive labor costs. (It takes longer to install a Wi-Fi enabled Japanese toilet than the most basic model.)
- Tile can cost anywhere from $2 to $30 per square foot and up; there is ceramic and porcelain tile as well as natural stone. These all come with different labor costs, too.

If you are on a strict budget, you can see how easy it is to exceed your limit just through materials costs and possibly labor. If you still insist to move forward before all your finish selections are completed and compiled into a specification document, there are a few issues you should be aware of, too.

- Be prepared for a much more stressful construction project.
- Your GC has to give you a selection sheet* that notes the due date when you must make your final decision on each category of finish. If not, you can cause serious delays and failing to make final decisions might entail financial penalties too. (See Appendix F)

Planning is the key to success. Do you go on vacation without planning? Would you trek into the wilderness without a plan? NO, you wouldn't, so why would you want to start one of the most important and expensive decisions of your life without a clear detailed plan in place?

CHOOSING A GENERAL CONTRACTOR (GC)

It is not an exaggeration to say that choosing your general contractor will be one of the biggest decisions you make in your life. You and your GC will be attached at the hip from start to finish; you might even spend more time with them over the course of the construction project than with your spouse or family. Choosing the right person for the job is crucial for your sanity, happiness, and success. Believe me, there will be some suffering but a good GC can reduce the pain. I'm not trying to scare you. I just want you to have a good experience because after all the months of planning, waiting, delays, and dust you will want to have the satisfaction of enjoying the fruits of your labor without unnecessary suffering from hiring the wrong GC. Ultimately, you need to find a GC whom you trust, whom you get along with, who understands what you want from your project, and who can help you make decisions along the way and manage your expectations. A GC who does not have these abilities will make you miserable and your project will reflect this. Just because a GC is "a nice guy" doesn't mean they will be good. Even a GC who is scrupulously honest won't necessarily be the one who can finish your project.

A good GC will oversee and coordinate your project along with their subcontractors so the job runs smoothly and at least relatively on time. Hiccups along the way are inevitable but a good GC will minimize them.

When soliciting bids on a project, it is important to remember that GCs have specialties. Remodeling and new construction are two very different animals. But in places where the housing industry has slumped, some homebuilders will attempt to present themselves as remodeling experts. When judging a GC, it's important to look at their previous work and assess how similar it is to the job you'd like to do. [*Interestingly, I would argue that blank-slate construction of a new home is actually an easier task. Most GCs, even those who normally specialize only in renovations, could probably handle this kind of work with the right crew at the right price.*]

Don't be surprised if there are substantial variations in pricing. It is unfortunately common for some contractors to give a lowball estimate and make up the cost difference later on with change orders. Other GC firms are often minimally financially solvent. Choose the wrong one, and you might be left with an incomplete job because your GC has run out of money to pay their subcontractors or materials. Too many contractors pay for work done for their last client with money from their current client. The lowest bids will be low for a reason, and it's almost certainly not because that particular GC has magically found a way to do everything more cheaply.

So now let's talk about how you are going to find the right person for your construction job. Perhaps the architect you used to draw your plans has a GC whom they prefer to use. That is fine, but even so you need to get three bids *at a minimum*. (We'll talk more about bidding in the next chapter.) You might have a friend who did a construction project who has a GC to recommend. Maybe you have seen a construction company's sign in your neighborhood. If so, you could talk with the homeowners. In general, it's important to remember that a GC is only going to give you their positive references, so take the time to look up the contractor license with the state licensing board, your local building department, and the Better Business Bureau. Find previous clients of the GC's without asking them. Do your due diligence! This is a historically important decision you're making.

An interview is an essential part of the GC hiring process. Just as if you were interviewing the GC for a job at your office, ask questions and encourage them to ask questions too. Some good questions might include:

- Will the GC develop a schedule with deadlines for when your selections have to be chosen and give it to you at the beginning of the job? This is a big determinant of how smoothly the job will run.
- Who will supervise your job? Will it be a project manager (PM)* or the actual GC? If a PM, you should ask to meet them as well. Ask how often *they* will be onsite. If the GC or PM does not watch and run a job with purpose, solving problems as they arise, the problems will escalate and become catastrophes.
- How many jobs is the firm juggling at a time?
- Do they use the same subcontractors* (or "subs") for every project, or rebid for every project? <u>A good GC is only as good as their subcontractors</u>. Many people are understandably more comfortable using a larger GC firm, but it's important to remember that no matter the size of the construction company it will use subcontractors for many parts of the project. A GC that sticks with its subcontractors is a good sign that it can build healthy working relationships. You probably will meet most of the subs or at least the owner of the companies during the "sub walk*" (more on that under Bidding).

> I used the same subs on all my jobs for several reasons, but mainly because they did very good work. We all understood what was expected, we were used to working with each other, so it made us a more cohesive team, and they all gave me fair and competitive prices for their labor. I could probably have rebid for each new job and lowered the price of my services, but I believed in rehiring the same people for cohesiveness so long as they kept doing their work well and on time.

As always, you are your own best advocate. Your goal in the interview process should not just be to choose the most qualified GC, but also to ensure that someone other than you will solve the innumerable small problems that arise over the course of construction. Your interests and those of the GC are not inherently aligned. The GC is there to make money, but a GC who understands that the easiest way to do that is to run a project successfully is the one you'll want to hire.

Once more, let's summarize what to look for in a potential GC:

- A GC experienced in your type of construction project.
- A GC with whom you can have a good rapport. (This is not the same as one who will be your "best friend.")
- A GC who is a good communicator.
- A GC who understands the scope of the construction project.
- A GC who has very good subs and retains them from one job to the next.
- A GC or PM who commits to being onsite a good portion of the day or at least one who will visit frequently!

BIDDING

In this business, you get what you pay for. I cannot over emphasize this fact! The GC world is full of inexperienced or less than honest GC's who will submit low bids, then try to make up the difference in several ways, one of which is change orders during the construction. I would often talk myself blue in the face when explaining to prospective clients that our bidding process was more accurate and ultimately fairer (since we submitted a Fixed-Cost* rather than a Cost Plus* proposal) than just accepting the lowest bids. Even if the lower bids say they are fixed-cost remember their contract might have language in it that allows them to increase their price. Like "unforeseen circumstances" or "events beyond their control". Even I had these clauses in my contract. I just rarely if ever used them. Time and again, however, I found that people were willing to risk their dream home or renovation on a lower bid. The lower bids could be much lower. However, if the other bids you are reviewing are in a similar range, then you should ask yourself "why is that one bid lower?" What am I not seeing in the proposal?

> We were doing a job when Hurricane Katrina hit the South. All of a sudden all of the plywood got shipped to the hardest hit areas; the price skyrocketed and the relevant plywood was in short supply because there are only so many manufacturing facilities in the US.
>
> Another time there was a fire at a sheetrock factory and the price jumped because of the simple fact of supply and demand.

As I noted previously, in the bidding process you can ensure you receive more accurate and easily comparable bids from construction companies if you have more information to give them. Try to avoid using "allowances" as stand-ins on your budget rather than specific materials. Allowances can be deceptive when you do not yet know what individual items cost or you have a Ripple Wine budget but Champagne taste. If you must use allowances, make sure all the bidders use the same allowance numbers for the same line items.

I'll admit that most of the time I allowed my clients not to have their finishes chosen up front, since most of them did not know that was preferable. However, I made sure the clients had a selection sheet with due dates so that everything got chosen on time. I also worked with great showroom specialists who kept my clients to the budget that we had settled on.

There are three main ways for GCs to assess the cost of a construction project, which in turn determines the price they will bid:

Project comparison estimation means the GC will base their bid on personal experience with similar projects. It is not very accurate and in my opinion is truly a "guesstimate." This is not to say these estimates aren't sometimes correct, but I would exercise caution if a GC told me this was the method they were using.

Square foot estimation relies on more comprehensive historical databases maintained by some larger firms based on (you guessed it) the per-square-foot cost of previous jobs they have done. This kind of estimation cannot produce anything more accurate than a range, however, as square-foot costs can vary significantly depending on finish. It is a fast way to produce an estimate, but again not truly accurate.

Bid estimation is determined by what your direct construction costs are. These include subcontractor quotations, material quantity takeoffs that are quoted from the appropriate vendor, overhead, field supervision, and profit. I prefer bid estimation because of its accuracy. It involves the GC scheduling a "sub walk" (I've also heard it called a "sub party") which is a job site walkthrough conducted by the GC and their subs. Everyone has a set of plans and can see the site conditions and existing structure. The architect might be onsite as well. Based on the site visit the subs will put together a bid for their portion of the work. It is a labor-intensive process, especially when you consider that this is *before* the awarding of the contract. On the other hand, it allows the GC to present the client with a proposal that incorporates *specific* costs, essentially locking both parties into one price. In the long run, I believe this method benefits everyone involved. Moreover, the walkthrough gives you as a client an idea of who the subs will be, how they will interact with you, and how professional they are.

> I was once asked to give an estimate for constructing a new house. The preliminary drawings were very elaborate. I submitted my preliminary bid of 1.2 million. (For my company a preliminary bid would consist of giving the potential client a price range based on estimating the average cost of products and speaking and showing the plans to the subs about the project.) I was told by the client that they had another bid of $400,000 to build the entire house. I told them that the material costs alone would exceed $400,000. This project was destined to failure and unrealized expectations.

PROPOSALS

Below are two proposal examples: one somewhat general, the other more detailed. Comparing the two examples will give you an idea of what to look for in a good proposal. The formatting may be different, but what is important is that they should include the key points. You might need to create a checklist so you can thoroughly compare the different proposals/bids. Remember, you should assume that nothing is included if it is not in the proposal—even if the GC tells you in person that it is. As with anything this important in life, get it in writing!

Below is what a roughly estimated proposal using allowances and generalities might look like. A proposal is a good way to work through most of the specifics. If we could agree on the proposal, then I would draw up a more detailed contract. I found that clients tended to like the list format because it is easier to understand, but a GC might not make theirs as easy to decipher.

NAME OF COMPANY

DATE:
LOCATION:
OWNER:
ESTIMATED PRICE RANGE: $138,000.00 - $174,500.00

The following are included in the estimate:

1. New 16' x 20' two-story addition per architectural plans
2. All framing with 2x4s
3. Bat fiberglass insulation
4. Electrical per drawing
5. Drywall
6. Relocation of some existing ductwork and new second floor HVAC system
7. Windows in the new addition and skylight in existing bathroom
8. Exterior foundation to be brick veneer
9. Exterior upper to be siding
10. All closets to have shelf and one pole
11. 5x7 Master closet w/ no shelving
12. Interior doors to be two panel w/ Ogee
13. Interior trim
14. New 25 year shingle roof on addition
15. Two new full baths
16. Ceramic
17. Finished oak hardwood
18. Paint interior and exterior
19. Clean debris from yard
20. Broom-swept interior

Now read proposal example no. 2, which includes specific finishes and a hard price:

NAME OF COMPANY

DATE:
LOCATION:
OWNER:
PRICE: $162,785.00

The following are included in the estimate:

1. New 16' x 20' two story addition per architectural plans
2. All framing with #2 grade wood 2x4s
3. Fiber glass bat insulation per drawings
4. Electrical per drawings and to code
5. Drywall to be ½ inch through out with tub surround to be ½ Durock*
6. Relocation of 20ft of 6x10 ductwork and new second floor 2-½ ton 16 seer Carrier HVAC system.
7. JELD-WEN low-E windows in the new addition and a Velux 14-1/2 x 45-3/4 Tempered Low E3 No Blind skylight in existing bathroom. Model FS A06 2005
8. Exterior foundation per plans will be brick veneer to match existing house MACAP*
9. Exterior siding per plans will be smooth, pre-primed 6 ½" fiber cement board with 5" exposure.
10. All closets to have one pressboard shelf and one 1" wood dowel pole.
11. 5x7 Master closet w/ no shelving
12. Interior doors to be solid core wood veneer two panel w/Ogee
13. Interior trim to MACAP
14. Soffit and fascia to be fiber cement board
15. New 25-year architectural shingle roof on addition with galvanized drip edge
16. Two new full baths to include one toilet, one sink and one bathtub in each
17. Ceramic to be laid on a horizontal pattern
18. Select 2 ½ red oak hardwood w/ two coats water base semi-gloss finish in all areas except bathrooms and master bedroom
19. $3,000 allowance for permits
20. $2,000 allowance for plumbing fixtures
21. $2,000 allowance for ceramic
22. $1,500 allowance for two bath vanities and two countertops
23. $300 allowance for mirrors
24. Exterior two-coats of Sherwin Williams exterior Resilience
25. Interior one coat primer and two-coats Sherwin Williams Duration
26. Seed and straw disturbed areas in the yard
27. Professional house cleaning at end of job

The following are not included in the estimate:

27. Carpet (by others)
28. Surface mounted lights (OPCI*)
29. Towel bars (OPCI)
30. Underground utilities
31. New water service
32. New electrical panel
33. Window treatments

Continued on next page.

The following are not included in the estimate and are considered alternates:

- $36,500 for building a new 9' x10' screen porch, adding a door into dining room, and enclosing the existing screen porch with full JELD-WEN low-E windows and exterior door.

- $1,500 for installation of Select 2 ¼ red oak hardwood in master bedroom sanded and finished with two coats of water base semi-gloss sealer.

It should be fairly obvious by comparing both proposals, which one starts to give you a better idea of what you will be getting. As well, the second proposal allows you to ask more pertinent questions, too. However, the proposals you might look at could be much harder to decipher.

CONTRACTS

Contracts, alternate pricing,* and change orders* are critical aspects of construction work. Let me say first of all that I am not an attorney and nothing in this book constitutes professional legal advice. There are three main types of construction contracts which I briefly explain below. However, these are merely synopses and are not comprehensive in anyway and there are many variations of these contracts.

Fixed Price/Lump Sum contract where the total cost is fixed. This works well when there is a clearly defined scope of work and a well-developed time schedule.

Cost Plus contract can be used when the scope of work is not clearly defined. Actual construction cost and expenses are itemized and billed to the client. There usually is a fixed percentage of the materials and labor pre-negotiated to cover overhead expenses.

Time and Material contract can also be used when the scope is not clearly defined. The two parties must agree to a daily or hourly rate plus material cost. In this case costs need to be clearly classified.

Once again, the better defined the scope of work is, the smoother the project will be on all levels. I would, however, like to draw your attention to some important points that should be addressed and made clear in any contract you enter.

Remember to always read your contract thoroughly. It might be prudent to have an attorney specializing in construction to read the contract before signing as well. Avoid entering into a "black hole contract" which is vague, includes little or no specifications, and will only lead to headache (see Appendix G). Make sure that all materials and finishes are clearly specified in the document, where possible. A good contract should also include supporting documents such as blueprints, shop drawings, specification sheets, etc. The purpose of these items is to leave nothing in doubt for either party. My philosophy about a good contract is that it is like the owner's manual of your car: you should make sure it's there when you buy it, but you should never have to look at it again. However, if there is a dispute, your contract is the document that governs the expectations, the method of change, and often the method of dispute resolution.

I have included in this book a copy of 2 old contract templates I used. These are examples, but are not intended for your use, and are provided solely as examples. The first is a shorter contract that was used for smaller projects (Appendix H) and a longer more detailed one that was used for larger and more complicated projects (Appendix I). Check with you local building department, or the state's contracting board, to make sure that they do not require a specific contract, clauses or language for their jurisdiction. However, let me point out some key points that you should consider in a contract:

Contractor responsibilities. For example, the GC's duties to *you*.

Warranty. Is there one? How long does it last? What does it cover?

Owner's responsibilities. *Your* duties to the GC. In my contracts, this basically says "don't bother the subs and let them do their work". It might also set deadlines for timely selection of materials if you haven't chosen them already. (But I know that this will not be you!)

Timeline (calendar). How long the project is expected to take to complete. As you might expect, this section would probably not name a hard-and-fast date in order to account for unforeseen circumstances. However, it should not give the GC free rein either.

Payment or Draw Schedule. This will specify when payments to the GC are made. It is important to make sure you withhold a significant amount of money until the GC finishes the job. Everyone has heard horror stories about incomplete jobs or jobs that never happened after the GC was given a substantial amount of money. A fair draw schedule will factor in the GC's liability as relates to upfront costs, such as whether or not the GC or the client is purchasing materials. It will also incorporate performance indicators, such as passing inspections and completing specific tasks like framing, plumbing, drywall, *etc*. I have included here a hypothetical draw schedule to guide you. (Note that GCs may run a different draw schedule with their own subs based on an internal incentive system, within legal limits of course. If a sub complains to you that they haven't been paid, your reply should be to take it up with the GC. Don't be pressured into acting as an arbitrator!)

> Recently I hired a guy to install some pavers. He told me that he wanted 50 percent of the agreed-upon price up front. Noting that I was supplying the materials and thus he had no upfront costs, I refused. All he had to do was pay one or two men's wages for the day and gas money. (Even if he *were* supplying materials, 50 percent is an absurd amount to pay anyone up front.) Instead, I proposed an initial draw on the first day he was on site working, a second after he was halfway done, and the rest on completion. He agreed and began work. Towards the end of the project, which in my estimation would require one more day's work, he asked for the majority of the final payment. I told him he could finish the following day and then I would pay him as we had initially agreed. He told me he had to start another job the next day so he would not be able to finish the next day but he promised to come back and finish after he finished the next job. I told him if he did not finish the next day that he would not be receiving his last payment. He could start his next job after he finished mine. It was not my fault that he did not schedule his time appropriately. This is a big red flag: If I had given him money in most likelihood, I would never have seen him again. My feeling is that he just did not want to finish the job. However, since I had withheld enough money, he had financial incentive to come back and finish, which he did. You should not be inconvenienced based on his inability to schedule properly or manage his finances.

Whatever you do, avoid a GC who asks for advances on their payments. You are not a bank—your job is not to lend your GC money. If your GC desperately needs the money sooner than scheduled, find another GC!

Here is a sample draw schedule based on an incentive system:

Initial Deposit =	$ upon signing the contract
Second Draw =	$ upon commencement of construction
Third Draw =	$ upon completion and passed inspection of framing
Fourth Draw =	$ when windows are substantially set
Fifth Draw =	$ upon commencement of plumbing rough-ins
Six Draw =	$ upon commencement of electrical rough-ins
Seventh Draw =	$ upon successful concealment inspection* (plumbing, electrical and HVAC)
Eighth Draw =	$ when sheetrock is hung
Ninth Draw =	$ when tile is installed
Tenth Draw =	$ when hardwood floor is installed
Eleventh Draw =	$ upon successful final inspection
Final Payment =	$ upon completion of final punch list and signing of all lien waivers.

Protection of Persons and Property. The GC must provide supervision, ensure workers' safety, protect the job site from loss, and abide by applicable laws, ordinances, and regulations.

Insurance and Bonds. The contractor must have General Liability insurance and Workmen's Compensation Insurance. I will discuss this in fuller detail later under insurance. As well, sometimes a contractor will be bonded. This means that the contractor has purchased a surety bond, which is a type of insurance that protects the homeowner if work is not completed.

Changes in the Work. This article should outline how the process of implementing change orders (CO) will work during the course of the construction project. Many state laws and regulations require a specific method of documenting change orders. The primary way is that BEFORE the work is done, the contractor provides you with a change order that describes the additional work that is to be done, any changes in the cost of the work, and any changes in the contract completion date. This needs to be signed before the work is done. Sometimes this information may not be complete and it will need to be updated. But you and the contractor need to make this joint decision before the work is started. The GC has the duty to provide you with an accurate CO and you have the duty to reasonably review and approve CO's. I usually gave my clients 3 options for determining how we would handle the pricing of COs:

- by mutual acceptance of a lump sum properly itemized.
- by unit prices or allowances stated in the Contract Documents or subsequently agreed upon.
- by time and materials cost itemized and supported by time records and material invoices plus 15% overhead and 15% profit.

Correction of Work. In this clause the contractor agrees to correct deficient, defective, or nonconforming work within a certain agreed upon period.

Termination of the Agreement. This is a more complicated series of clauses that allows either party to basically call it quits (terminate the contract). This could include, for example, lack of payment (owner), not following the contract (either party), not having access to the jobsite (owner), lack of progress (GC), not provided selections of materials or finishes etc. (owner).

The Specification List. We spoke about creating this list in an earlier chapter and it should be part of your contract documents and included in the contract appendix

Drawings. All drawings should be part of the contract documents as part of the appendix.

ALTERNATE PRICING

I always told my clients to shoot for the stars and if the costs were prohibitive then we would cut back on the finishes or scale of the project. I also suggested that we could provide "alternate pricing*" (AP) for them. This is when you provide a price for an additive or subtractive element (a credit). An example of an additional cost is substituting different materials such as (Red Oak vs. White Oak flooring), or something on a larger scope would be enclosing a screen porch. An example of a credit could be carpet in lieu of hardwood.

You do not necessarily have to decide at that moment on the change; you can wait until after construction has started. Of course, all changes will need to be decided and executed before they affect your schedule. These can be added to your finish schedule calendar so you will easily be reminded. The AP document(s) should be included with the contract documents as an appendix.

The reason for specifying AP in the beginning is twofold:

- First, it is easier to have the subcontractors determine AP while they are calculating their bid at the beginning of the job rather than midway through it.
- Second, it is faster to initiate the change order should one be necessary because the pricing and specifications will have been determined beforehand.

Here are three examples of AP language. AP can be additive or subtractive to the original contract amount.

> 1) $1,500 for the installation of Select 2 ¼ red oak hardwood sanded and finished with 2 coats of water base semi-gloss sealer in lieu of carpet in master bedroom. *In this case the carpet was not in the original pricing: the material was supplied and installed by others so there is no "credit" given for the carpet.*

2) $800 for material and installation of porcelain laid in a horizontal pattern (should have description/product number of material to be used) in lieu of ceramic laid in a horizontal pattern in the guest bathroom. *In this case the difference is more expensive material and labor from the base price given in the proposal.*

3) ($1,200) for Type II granite in lieu of Type III granite in the kitchen. *In this case there is a credit given for using a less expensive material. The labor usually does not change based on type of granite.*

CHANGE ORDERS (COs)

No one likes change orders, but they are an inevitable part of home construction work. You can minimize them by endeavoring to make as many of the design and material decisions as possible before work begins. Most COs occur as a result of an issue that arises on site due to unforeseen circumstances such as accommodation of unexpected site conditions once a home's internal structure is exposed. A CO would also be issued in the event that the GC and the client decide to revert to one of the AP schemes outlined in the contract. Change orders are *not* a tool for a GC to collect more money for the *same* work because they miscalculated the appropriate amount for that portion of the job, though a bad GC might use them for this purpose.

> We were finishing a basement project that included adding a new bedroom, bathroom, and laundry room. This meant we had to add a new waste line to the existing one under the concrete floor, which in turn meant we had to dig up part of the concrete floor to tie into the existing main sewer line. When we opened up the floor, the plumber noticed a lot of standing water. He called me and we determined that the main sewer line had rusted through under the concrete slab. Who knows how long the waste had just been percolating under their basement floor? (Pretty gross isn't it?) When I told the homeowners, the wife broke out crying. It was not a very comfortable situation, but sometimes as a GC I had to be the bearer of bad news. We first drew up a CO to run a camera through the sewer and determine what course of action needed to be taken. Then we made a second change order for digging up the sewer line up to the exterior wall and replacing it, then inserting a sleeve into the existing sewer line from the house to the street. The sleeving saved the homeowners some money in the end and the good news was that we were able to fix a serious problem while the basement was still unfinished. However, it did delay the project by three weeks and admittedly was expensive.

Change orders come in many formats, but what is most important is that the CO be *specific*. This is to say, it should elaborate in detail:

- The specifications of the change.
- The materials needed to execute the change, and their associated costs.
- The amount of time the change is expected to take.
- When the new work will begin and end.
- Whether a change in the final completion date of the project is expected.
- What the payment schedule for the new work will be.

For an example of what a Change Order might look like, see Appendix J.

INSURANCE

Because many things can go wrong on a job site, it is important to make sure you and your GC have the necessary insurance coverage. Have your GC contact their insurance company and add your name to their General Liability Insurance as a "certificate holder." Then have the insurance company email or mail it to you. Do not accept it from the GC directly. In most states your GC needs workmen's compensation insurance. If it is required and the GC does not have the insurance then you may be liable for injuries to the GC's employees. This coverage will appear on the Certificate of Insurance. It might be a good idea to have copies of the subcontractors' insurance certificates too. Make sure none of their policies are expired—you may even want to call the insurance agencies to confirm. It will take five minutes of your time and, should the worst happen, could save you thousands. Unfortunately, it is not uncommon in the construction industry for contractors to let their insurance policies lapse or claim that they are covered under someone else's policy. Also, you should know that most insurance policies do not cover defective or bad work.

You should also make sure your homeowner's insurance protects you from liability. Construction Risk Policies insure the part of the property under construction. Your homeowner's policy might cover this, but you should be absolutely sure that it does. Who is responsible for the insurance is very important. If you agree to purchase Construction Risk Insurance and fail to do so, then you may have to become the insurer.

You might want to consider taking out your own Builders Risk insurance policy as well. Talk to your insurance agent and describe the scope of the project, then see if they quote a reasonable price. It might not be necessary, but it could be useful if the cost is not burdensome. The important thing is to make an informed decision and understand your risk! Seek advice from your insurance agent.

For an example of what a certificate of insurance document will look like, see Appendix K. Your name and address should appear under Certificate Holder. Workers compensation is included on the Certificate too. Note the coverage amounts.

PERMITS

I cannot emphasize one point enough: **do not attempt to obtain (or "pull" in construction parlance) any of your own permits.** If a GC suggests you do so, find a new GC. While it is true that you may save a bit of money (since you're contributing your labor rather than your GC's labor to the process), it is not worth it for you. Your GC and their subcontractors should pull all their own permits. In most jurisdictions, in fact, they are the only people who will be allowed to do so. The reason is that it keeps the GC and subcontractors liable, rather than you. This way, if there are ever inspection issues the building department will put pressure on the offender (i.e. not you) rather than on you.

This is not to say that you should not inquire about the status of your permits. Quite the opposite. Ask your GC for the reference numbers—in most cases these days, you should be able to track their progress online. Having pulled the necessary permits, your GC will then post them on a board or the window of the construction site.

On a cautionary note: shadier GCs and tradesmen will even resell access to their trade licenses to enable unlicensed workers to obtain permits (this is, of course, illegal). Don't let it happen to you!

INSPECTORS AND INSPECTIONS

The building inspectors whom I met in my career varied substantially in their skills and knowledge. Some had previously worked in a building trade themselves, while others had done it their entire career. All of them, of course, had passed an exam to become building inspectors. What I learned quickly, however, is that it is hard, if not impossible, for anyone to actually know all aspects of the International Building Code. (I certainly don't either—part of the logic of having subcontractors is that by their specialized nature they will know their relevant sections of the IBC* better than I ever could.) Add to that the fact that the 2018 IBC book is 726 pages long and changes with some regularity.

There is a fine line on how much a GC can—and should—push back against the building inspectors. Ultimately, they are there to make sure your project is constructed according to code and possibly to be helpful. But GCs also should have your interest at heart, insofar as they can argue for aspects of the project that follow the spirit of the IBC if not the exact letter, in order to save you grief and money. Obviously one would not want to do this with every element of a project or even the majority, but it is important to keep in mind that the IBC intends for every project to be built to a standard that can exceed what is necessary for public safety. Just as highway engineers tend to design roads so that even the person going 25 miles per hour above the speed limit is still fairly safe, so too can the IBC recommend "over engineering."

> In any event, I found in my career a wide range of inspectors. One would simply ask me if I had done such-and-such rather than go look at it himself. When I said yes—truthfully, mind you—he gave me the "Passed" sticker. I even had an inspector who would drive up in his vehicle and I would go out and lolly gag with him about this and that. He would always ask if I had completed the item for inspection. I would answer yes and he would give me the passed sticker.
>
> There was another inspector I dealt with, however, that would actually carry the IBC book with him just to make sure I knew he was the boss. He would always be carrying the international codebook just in case you dared question him on what he said. He would open the book to the right page, and point at the section, and read it aloud to me. It was impressive. Another inspector once failed me on a groundwork plumbing inspection, even though he could not name anything violating the IBC that we had done. When he attempted to fail us a second time upon re-inspection, I appealed and was successful.

These stories notwithstanding, inspections are not hard to pass if your GC is conscientious and detail-orientated. A good GC monitors the progress of their subcontractors and should never schedule an inspection without themselves having inspected the work. I was always on-site for inspections, met the inspector with the approved set of plans, and walked with the inspector through the jobsite for the entire inspection. In many cases I would make sure a particular subcontractor whose work was being inspected was on-site as well. I should say that even if your project *does* fail inspection, it does not mean the GC and subcontractors are not doing an excellent job. In many cases, it is just impossible to predict what tiny faults the inspector might find.

The one lesson you should remember is that the Inspector is not necessarily there for you even though they should be. If you see a potential problem with the work, and your GC tells you that it has to be correct because the building inspector approved it, you might want to further investigate.

HOPPING ON THE ROLLER COASTER: STARTING YOUR PROJECT

Now you are at the point where you have approved building plans (after possibly a few revisions), you have hired a great GC, and are ready to start some demolition and possibly preparation for a new foundation. Understandably, you will be anxious and nervous. One of the phenomena you will soon get used to, however, is what I like to call the "roller coaster" of home construction. I use this metaphor not to scare you, but to characterize how over the life of a construction project you will see quick progress, then slowdowns that seem to last an eternity, then quick progress again. Moreover, while some aspects of construction will have an instant "wow factor," others, though essential, will appear to the layman's eye as if nothing has been done. Here are a few important rules that I would recommend you follow during the actual construction process:

- Secure the jobsite. Though they may not look like it, many construction materials (e.g. copper) are extremely valuable and easy to steal. The site always needs to be locked up when people are not around. A lock box with a code is a good option so that workers can access the site whether or not you are there. For the same reason, get to know all of the subcontractors who will be working on-site.

- Establish a schedule of weekly meetings with your GC or PM to touch base, conduct any business either one of you might have, ask questions, and get updates about the project and budgets. It is very important to meet weekly on the budget if you have a cost plus contract or if you have allowances.

- Ask your GC if they can lead you on a walkthrough at key points during the construction process. This will allow you to make onsite decisions if needed based on your assessment of the actual physical structure and to keep tabs on the work being done.

- Whenever a product is delivered to the site, make sure it is immediately inspected and stored in a safe location. Too many times, I found that wrong products were delivered or the product was damaged (even if it did not appear to be from the outside).

    > I was renovating a kitchen once and when the cabinets were delivered none of the boxes showed any damage. When we went to open the first box, however, the cabinet was completely smashed. I assume that it was actually packed damaged.

- Maintain a chain of command by voicing your concerns directly with the GC or project manager rather than with the subcontractors. Many problems on my worksites arose because clients subverted the chain of command.

    > One time I had to leave town for a short period, and when I got back the owner had had the electrician wire a room in his basement for a full kitchen. No one had told me—the owner had told the subcontractor to just hand me a change order. Not only was this ridiculous, but now I was liable to the building department for having violated the approved building plans—even to the extent that I could have lost my license. I went to the chief building inspector and reported the incident, and told the owner that he was now responsible for revising the building plans and obtaining new permits. Though the owner broke the contract by instructing the subcontractor

to perform something not in the scope of the contract, the subcontractor was also at fault for not alerting me and subsequently performing the work without a signed change order.

LIFE ON THE ROLLER COASTER:
A GENERAL OUTLINE OF THE CONSTRUCTION PROCESS

What follows is a general outline of the construction process. Depending on the scope of your work, it or its sequencing might change slightly depending on your GC and your building codes.

- ☐ Groundwork
- ☐ Preparation for footing
- ☐ Inspection
- ☐ Pouring of footing
- ☐ Survey (check to make sure footing does not encroach on the setbacks)
- ☐ Start of foundation
- ☐ Framing**
- ☐ Installation of water-resistant material on roof
- ☐ Wall bracing
- ☐ Installation of windows
- ☐ HVAC rough in**
- ☐ Plumbing rough in**
- ☐ Electrical rough in**
- ☐ Close-in inspection of plumbing/HVAC/electrical and framing
- ☐ Installation of finish roof
- ☐ Installation of siding
- ☐ Insulation
- ☐ Installation of drywall
- ☐ Completion of drywall
- ☐ Installation of flooring/tile
- ☐ Installation of cabinets
- ☐ Installation of doors and trim (casing and base board)**
- ☐ Painting
- ☐ Installation of appliances
- ☐ Punch list

The term *rough-in* means the trades (plumbing, electrical, HVAC subcontractors) have completed the first phase of their jobs. The plumbing pipes are run, sealed and secured; the bathtubs and shower pans are installed. The electrical cable is run and connected to the electrical panel, sub panel,* all electrical boxes, and recessed lights. There are no other devices installed. The HVAC unit is placed and all ductwork installed, sealed, secured, and insulated were applicable.

The *double asterisk* indicates steps at which you should perform a walkthrough with your GC and relevant subcontractor.

Framing
In my experience, framers can work extremely fast. Generally this is good for your project but sometimes can result in walls quickly getting built in the wrong location or walls that are not plumb,* depending on the competence of the crew foreman. I suggest measuring the room dimensions and double-checking them against the plans on your own time, when the workers are not there (it's safer for you, and you won't slow them down).

If you think there are issues or you see something that concerns you, then contact the GC and request a walkthrough with them. It is easier for the framers to make corrections as they go along than to have to redo work when they are already far into the project. (This is a general rule, but is particularly relevant for framing.)

Plumbing
Walk through and make sure that the rough-ins for all of your fixtures seem to be in the correct locations. Are all of the valves for the shower installed? The latest shower designs can be very complicated, depending on which model you chose. Are the rough-ins set to allow for the correct depth of your ceramic tile, natural stone, or porcelain? Have the workers protected the tub from damage?

Electrical
I would advise that your GC have the electrician hang all the electrical boxes (for outlets, switches and surface-mounted lights, the housings for the recessed lights, bath fans) before pulling any wire. I would then do a very careful walkthrough with the GC and the electrician (this is a walkthrough you cannot afford to miss). In detail I would discuss the location of each and the specific switches in each box. This way, if you need to make changes it is easily done.

Doors
Your GC should mark the door swing on the end side of the rough door opening so you understand during the walkthrough how your doors will function. It does not cost a penny to change the door swing before the doors are ordered.

These four walkthroughs allow you to easily make changes to improve the final product and will help ensure that fewer problems emerge at the end.

Just a quick note: there are 5 levels of drywall finishing. I will not go into full detail here, but I have included a general summary of the levels and where they are generally used in construction (see Appendix K). You can find more detailed and specific guidelines on the internet. As a general rule level 4 is sufficient for most painted surfaces. However, if you are applying semi-gloss or gloss you might want to look at level 5.

MOVING IN…NOT QUITE YET

So you just had your final inspection. Maybe you passed, or maybe you failed, but only have some small changes to make. In either case, now is time to give the GC their final punch list. There are several more steps before you can finalize your project, and hopefully say goodbye to your GC forever!

I used to say to my clients at this stage, "The only phone call I want from you is an invitation to dinner." After all of these years I never once was invited to dinner! On the other hand, in ten years of independent contracting I only had two post-completion calls from clients. One was cracked caulk in the corner of a shower, the other a missing brick between the fascia and the wall. No one ever requested warranty service, either. I briefly worked for another, larger contractor and they had an employee whose sole job was to do warranty work (i.e. going around and fixing all the mistakes his colleagues had made).

THE PUNCH LIST (OR, THE FINAL HURDLE TO SALVATION)

This is the last hurdle and it should not be too painful for either party. It is important that you carefully create the punch list. I would instruct my clients to come up with a list on their own, then I would write one too and we would compare. We would negotiate a final list, and would then sign it with the stipulation that neither party could subsequently add anything to the list (believe me, every client will find something they want to add to the list)(See Appendix M). Once this list is satisfactorily completed, your GC should give you all of the signed <u>lien waivers</u> and you will hand the GC their final check.

LIENS AND LIEN WAIVERS

If a GC or subcontractor provides construction or renovation services to you and is not paid, they can place a lien on your property. This usually has to be done within 90 days of the last day of the month the subcontractor performed work, depending on the state. The GC (or whoever places the lien) is not necessarily obligated to inform you—many homeowners only become aware of a lien when a title search is done in preparation to sell their house. A GC's reasons for placing a lien are not always honest. Perhaps they don't have the funds to pay their subcontractors, and intend to pay them using a portion of the value of your home. If a lien is filed against your property it is a good time to hire an attorney.

The purpose of a lien waiver is contained in the name: it is a document wherein the GC and the subcontractors confirm that they have been paid fully and waive their ability to place a lien on the property listed. You will need a separate lien waiver for the GC and for each subcontractor that worked on your home. (See Appendix N)

AFTERWORD

My purpose in writing this guide was to present a thorough step-by-step guide to familiarize the reader with the various phases of construction, its language and key documents to help protect you and your investment. As well to give the reader some helpful tips on how to hire the right general contractor for the job. Of course, each construction project has its own idiosyncrasies, and it would be presumptuous and inaccurate to claim that every situation you might encounter is discussed here. Think of these pages like your drawings: as a rudder to guide you through the vast sea that is the construction process. Though I would not recommend citing this work directly when you are in negotiations with your GC (there are few GCs out there who appreciate the feeling of being lectured by a former colleague), I truly believe that following the above mentioned suggestions will help your project run more smoothly and successfully.

APPENDIX

A) Sample Floor Plan

B) Sample Elevation

C) Sample Wall Section

D) Sample Wall Section Detail

E) Sample of Specifications

F) Sample Selection Guide

G) Sample "Black Hole Contract"

H) Sample Short Form Owner Contractor Agreement

I) Sample Comprehensive Contract

J) Sample Change Order

K) Sample Certificate of Insurance

L) Sample Drywall Finish Levels

M) Sample Punch List

N) Sample Lien Waiver

APPENDIX A

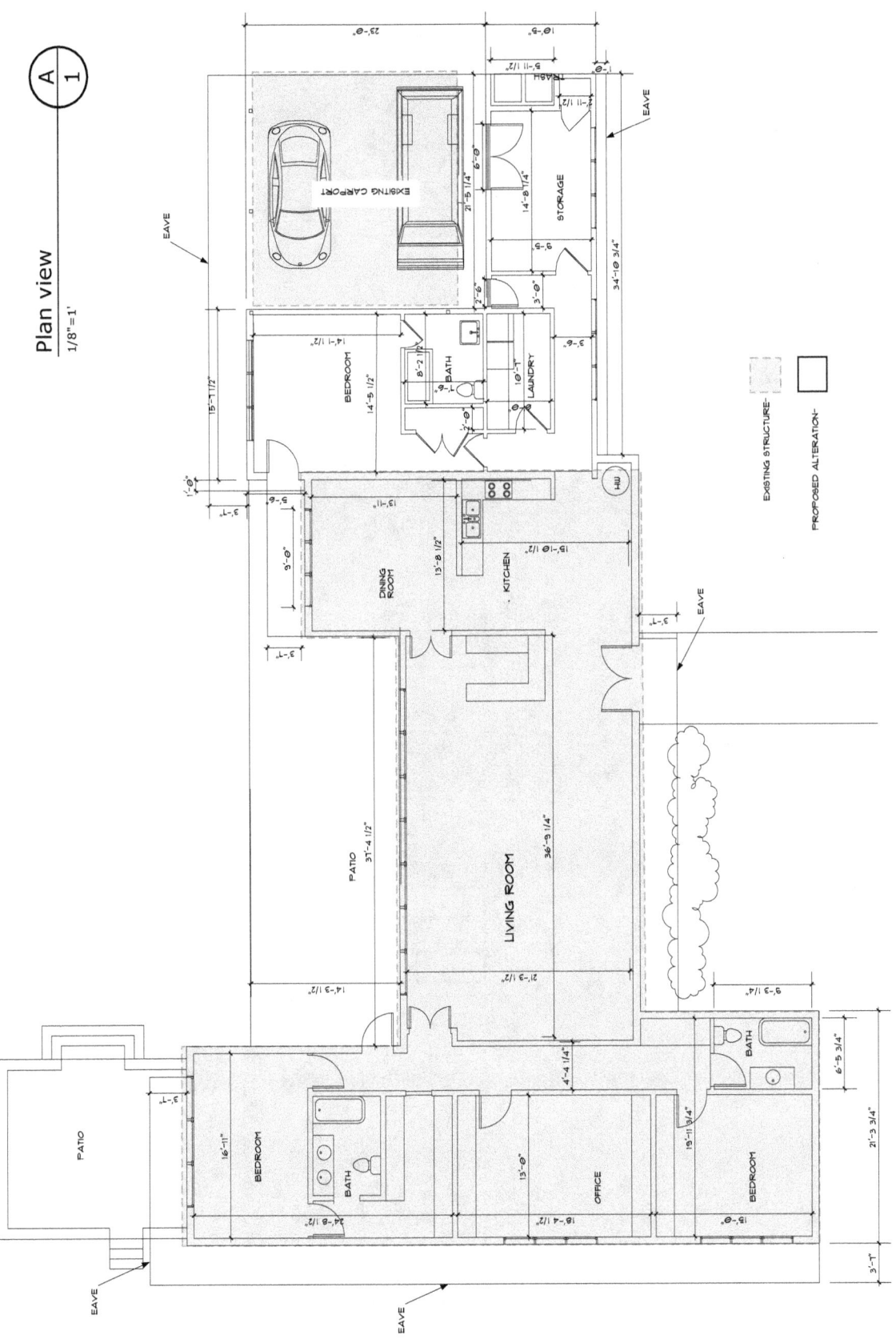

APPENDIX B

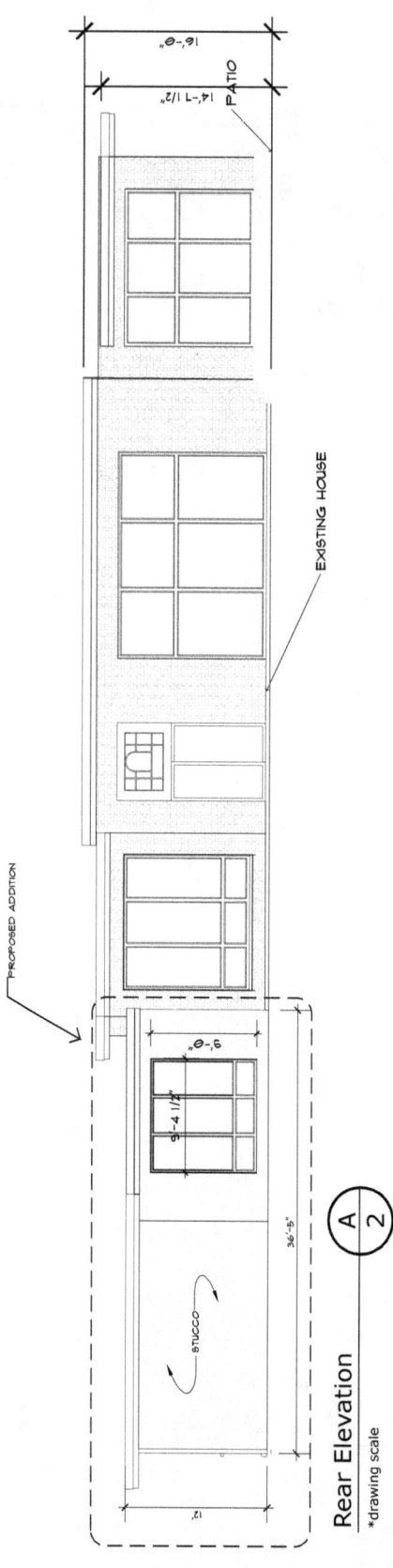

Rear Elevation
*drawing scale

APPENDIX C

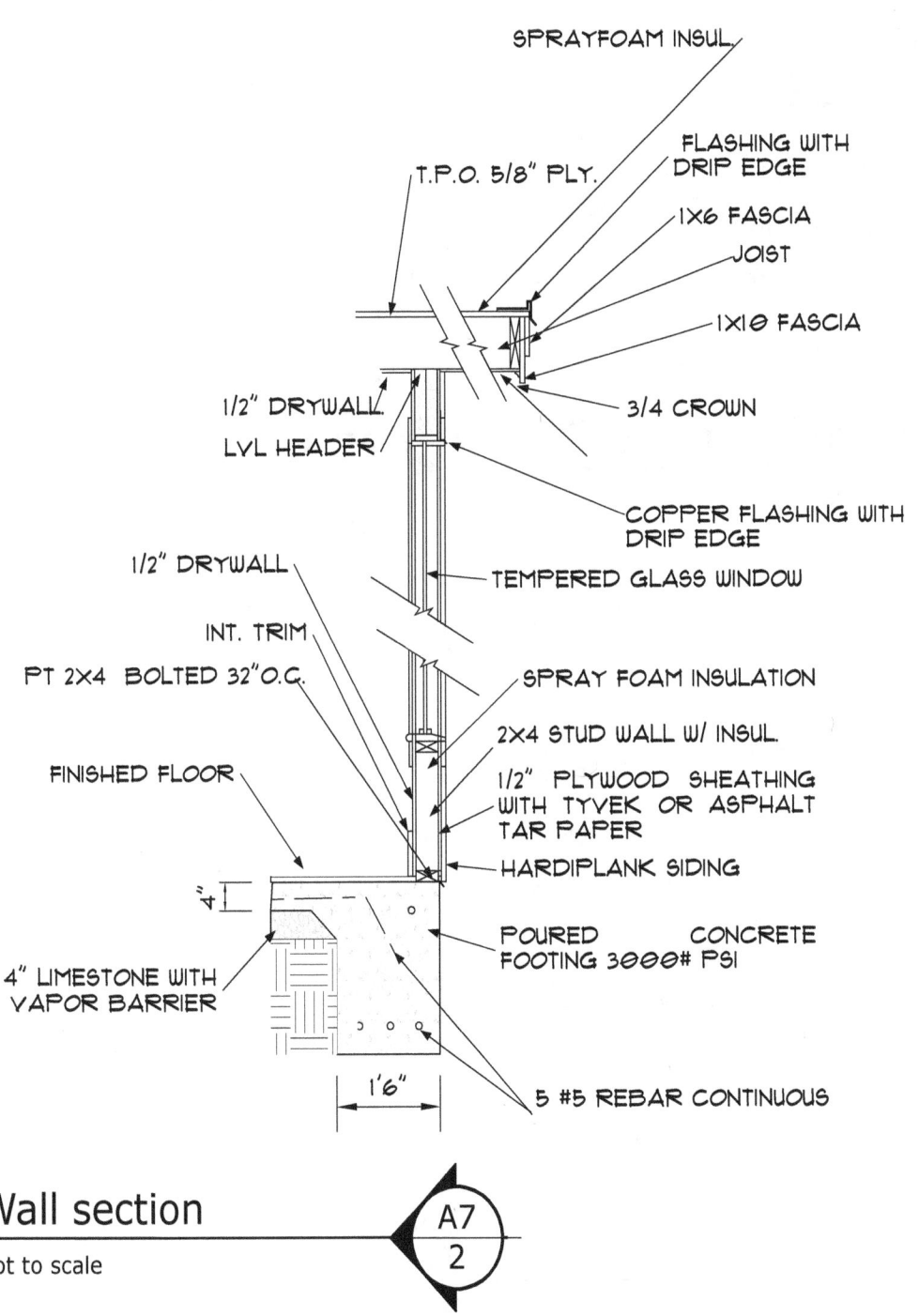

Wall section
not to scale

APPENDIX D

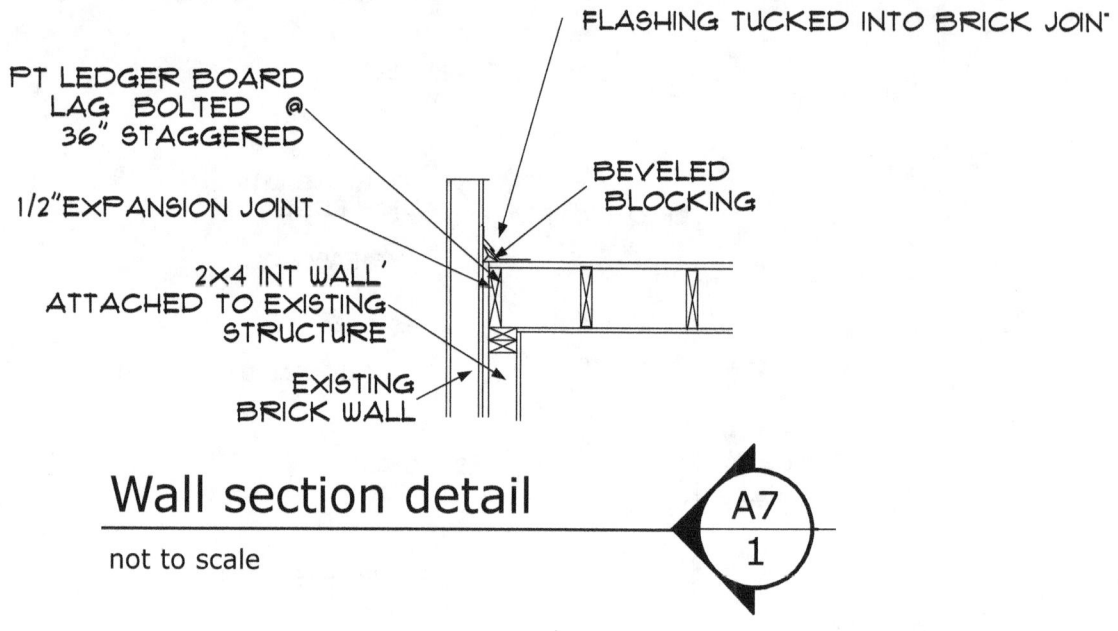

Wall section detail — not to scale — A7/1

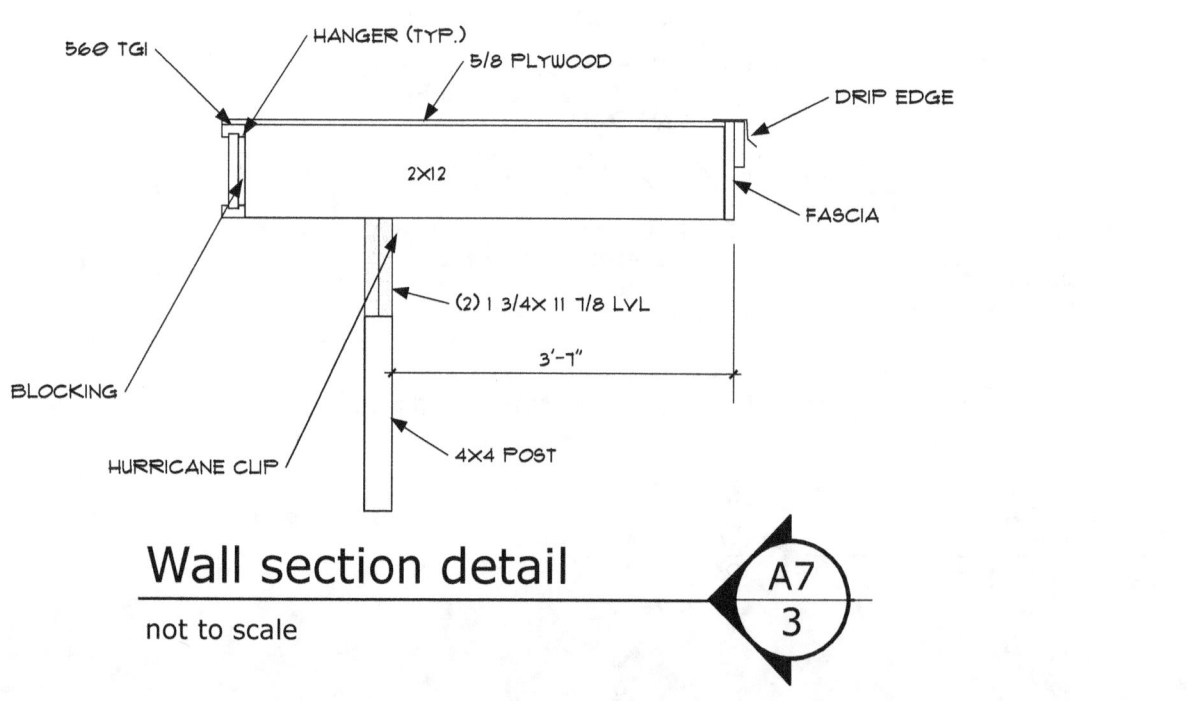

Wall section detail — not to scale — A7/3

APPENDIX E

SPECIFICATIONS
GENERAL
DEMOLITION
EXCAVATION
GRADING
DRIVEWAY
SITE WORK
CONCRETE

EXTERIOR
Masonry such as mortar/brick
Siding, Fascia
Windows, skylights and doors
Roofing
Gutters

MILLWORK
Molding, interior trim, cabinets, doors.

FLOORING (this would include all the flooring through out the entire project)
Wood, tile, ceramic, stone, laminate, carpet etc.

WALL FINISHES
Paint, Wallpaper (walls, ceiling and trim of each room and exterior; include sheen*).

BATHROOMS
Fixtures, lights, mirrors, shower doors etc.

KITCHEN
Appliances, cabinets, hardware etc.

ELECTRICAL
Style and manufacture of the switches and outlets.

The specifications should be part of your contract documents. This is just a basic outline and can become much more detailed too. As you can start to tell the more detail you include the better off you and the GC will be in executing your project.

APPENDIX F

Add due dates were applicable.

- ☐ **Windows**
- ☐ **Moldings**
- ☐ **Doors**
  - ☐ Exterior
  - ☐ Interior
- ☐ **Siding**
- ☐ **Roofing**
- ☐ **Any other exterior finishes?**
- ☐ **Flooring**
  - ☐ Main house
  - ☐ Basement
  - ☐ Kitchen
  - ☐ Bathrooms
  - ☐ Porch(s)
  - ☐ Deck
  - ☐ Patio
- ☐ **Kitchen**
  - ☐ Appliances (must choose your before cabinets)
  - ☐ Cabinets
  - ☐ Counter top
  - ☐ Back splash
  - ☐ Cabinet pulls and/or handles (supplied by owner or SBO)
- ☐ **Bathroom(s)**
  - ☐ Toilet
  - ☐ Sink/cabinet/counter top
  - ☐ Faucet
  - ☐ Bathtub
  - ☐ Shower/ bath tub fixture(s)
  - ☐ Shower door
  - ☐ Medicine cabinet
  - ☐ Vanity light
  - ☐ Tile, porcelain, or stone (does the stone need to be sealed?)
  - ☐ Grout color
  - ☐ Towel bars etc. (SBO)
- ☐ **Paint colors for entire house**
  - ☐ Living room
  - ☐ Office
  - ☐ TV room
  - ☐ Kitchen
  - ☐ Bathrooms
  - ☐ Bedrooms

NOTE: Add specialty items such as home theater, in wall speakers in the house, internet (cat-6) Coax cable, etc.

APPENDIX G

DUNCE CONSTRUCTION COMPANY of NADA Inc.
Not just building homes. Destroying Relationships.

BUILDING CONTRACT

WE, THE UNDERSIGNED, have read the forgoing documents, prepared in duplicate, and accept them as correct and hereby acknowledge receipt of one copy for each party hereto.

THIS AGREEMENT, made this _____ day of _____, 20___, Dunce Construction of NADA Inc, hereinafter called "Contractor", and Billy Bob and Marta Out of Luck, hereinafter called the "Unfortunate Owners".

WITNESSETH: That the Contractor and Unfortunate Owner for the consideration hereinafter named agree as follows:

ARTICLE I.
The Contractor agrees to provide the materials as specified and to perform all the General Conditions of the Contract, the Specifications and the Drawings, (Specifications to be agreed upon by Contractor and Unfortunate Owner).
Job Location: _____.
Job Description: _____.
Materials: _____.

ARTICLE II.
The Contractor agrees that the work under this contract shall start upon the approval of the construction loan, and shall be substantially completed in 6 months here after.

ARTICLE III.
The Unfortunate Owner agrees to pay the contractor in current funds for the performance of the contract. This contract shall be cost plus 12% with a budget cap of $_____, and to make payments on a percentage of the completion basis.

ARTICLE IV.
Inclusions and exclusions in budget (see attached Specifications).
It is agreed that the completion of the work covered in this contract is contingent upon strikes, lockouts, delay of common carriers, laws or governments regulations or any other circumstances or conditions beyond the control of the Contractor. You, the Unfortunate Owner, may cancel this transaction at any time prior to midnight of the third business day after the due date of this transaction.

ARTICLE VI.
The Contractor and the Unfortunate Owner agree: The specifications and the Drawings, together with this agreement form the contract, as if hereto attached. The Contractor shall comply with all local codes, inspections and requirements for building permits. All cancellation rights of parties must be disclosed. Consult your attorney for any specific cancellation requirements. Any modification to this contact which changes the cost, materials, work to be performed, or the estimated completion date must be made in writing and signed by all parties. The Contractor and Unfortunate Owner for themselves, their successor, executers, administrator and assigns, hereby agree to the full performance of the covenants herein contained.

Mr. A. R. Dunce
Dunce Construction of NADA Inc.   Contractor
Address Unknown
From Another Planet
000-00-000   Owner
A Class A…

APPENDIX H

OWNER-CONTRACTOR CONSTRUCTION AGREEMENT

Owner(s): _____
_____ -

and the Contractor: **Name of construction company**

Contractor License # _____ (Exp. Date _____)

For the following Project Name/Location: _____ Date: _____

The following is a CONTRACT for materials and labor to be supplied by the Contractor at the request and order of the homeowner.

DESCRIPTION OF WORK TO BE PERFORMED:

Per plans and scope of work dated _____ attached hereto and incorporated herein by reference.

Work to start approximately the week of: _____.
Work to be substantially completed approximately the week of _____. Owner agrees that the start and completion dates are subject to the Terms and Conditions attached hereto, and the receipt of permits and owner supplied materials. If this Contract is not ratified on the date of presentation, the start and completion dates will be extended or postponed.

BUYER'S RIGHT TO CANCEL

If this agreement was solicited at or near your residence and you do not want the good or services, you may cancel this agreement by mailing a notice to the seller. The notice must say that you do not want the goods or services and must be mailed before midnight of the third business day after you sign the Contract. The notice must be mailed to the Contractor at the address listed above.

PAYMENT SCHEDULE

The estimated cost of the above work, complete in accordance with the above specifications is: $_____. Payment is due and payable immediately on the date upon which the following occur, interest shall accrue on any late payments at a rate of 1-1/2% per month:

DO NOT SIGN IN BLANK. HOMEOWNER IS ENTITLED TO COPY OF THE CONTRACT (INCLUDING ANY ADDENDA) AT THE TIME HE OR SHE SIGNS. REQUIRED IF ADDITIONAL TERMS ARE ON THE REVERSE SIDE: READ ADDITIONAL TERMS ON THE BACK BEFORE SIGNING.

The foregoing terms, specifications and conditions are satisfactory and hereby agreed to. You are authorized to work as specified and payment will be made as outlined above. Upon signing this agreement, the homeowner represents and warrants that he or she is the owner or the authorized agent of the aforesaid premises and that he or she has read this agreement.

Contractor Name
Salesperson (Printed Name)   Homeowner (Printed Name)

VA or DC License #   Signature

_____   _____
Signature of Authorized Agent   Homeowner (Printed Name)

_____   _____
Date   Signature

                                                              _____
                                                              Date

This Contract may be withdrawn if not accepted by the Contractor within ____ business days.

TERMS AND CONDITIONS

GENERAL TERMS: For the purpose of these Terms and Conditions, the Owner is the person(s) or entity identified on page one of this form, and Silver Hammer Design + Construction, L.L.C. is the Contractor (hereinafter "Contractor"). This proposal for services shall be considered withdrawn if not signed and returned within thirty (30) days of the date hereof. If Owner fails to execute the attached proposal for services, performance of services shall be governed by these terms and conditions.

PERFORMANCE OF WORK: Contractor will endeavor to complete the work under this contract within the schedules set forth herein. Any delays caused by events beyond the control of Contractor shall not constitute abandonment and shall not be included in calculation time frames for payment or performance. Contractor shall reasonably comply with all state and local building codes and requirements for permits, inspections and zoning. Any modification to this contract which changes the scope, cost, materials, or the estimated completion date, must be made in writing and signed by all parties. Such change will be considered an addendum to this contract, subject to all stipulations of the original contract.

ACCESS TO PREMISES: Unless otherwise stated, Owner will provide Contractor with full access to the site for activities necessary for the performance of the services. The Owner understands that actual field conditions may subsequently be found to vary from the assumptions, which in turn, may alter or increase the scope of the design and/or construction cost. Evaluation, investigations, on-site opinions, consultations, or written reports do not constitute a warranty or guarantee (either expressed or implied) of the adequacy of the premises and/or existing structures.

THE FEE/PAYMENT: Owner shall strictly comply with the payment schedule set forth herein. **Please make checks payable to SILVER HAMMER DESIGN + CONSTRUCTION, LLC.** NO CASH WILL BE ACCPEPTED. Unpaid accounts are subject to a monthly service charge of 1.5 percent (annual percentage rate of 18 percent) on the unpaid balance, at the sole discretion of Contractor. In the event any portion or the entirety of an account remains unpaid thirty (30) days after billing, Contractor may, at its sole option begin formal collection efforts, for which the Owner shall pay all costs, including reasonable attorney's fees.

CANCELLATION: If you do not want the goods or services as proposed in this contract, you may cancel this agreement by sending a notice to Contractor by certified return receipt mail. The notice must state that you do not want the goods or services as proposed. You must send the notice before midnight of the third business day after you sign this contract. Notwithstanding, in no event can this contract be cancelled if Contractor has commenced work.

WARRANTY: Contractor warrants that all home improvement work done pursuant to this Contract shall be of workmanlike quality, and shall be in accordance with applicable building codes and standard industry practices. Provided the Owner is in full compliance with this contract and its payment obligations, Contractor shall remedy any defects, excluding normal wear and tear, due to faulty workmanship which appears within a period of one (1) year from the date of Substantial Completion. With respect to materials and equipment, any warranty furnished by manufacturer's warranty will be provided to Owner. This express warranty is in lieu of and excludes any other warranty, express or implied or otherwise. This express warranty applies to the Owner only, and to no other party whatsoever.

SUBSTANTIAL COMPLETION: "Substantial Completion" as defined herein, is the date upon which the work is sufficiently complete in accordance with the contract so that the Owner can occupy or utilize the work or designated portion thereof, for the use for which it was intended.

CLEAN UP/PROTECTION: Contractor will provide dust protection as practical and shall use reasonable efforts to keep the premises free from accumulation of waste materials or rubbish caused by Contractor's operations. Movement or protection of Owner's personal property and belongings by Contractor personnel, if required, will be charged on a time and materials basis. Reasonable care will be taken, but Contractor shall not be responsible or liable for any damage or loss, if any.

STRUCTURAL WORK: Contractor reasonably assumes the existing structure schedule to remain is in good condition and will not require work except as specifically noted. Retention of any structural engineers and/or structural work/repairs, if required/specified, will be Owner's sole responsibility.

RISK ALLOCATION: IN RECOGNITION OF THE RELATIVE RISKS, REWARDS, AND BENEFITS OF THE PROJECT TO BOTH THE OWNER AND CONTRACTOR, THE RISKS HAVE BEEN ALLOCATED SUCH THAT THE OWNER AGREES THAT, TO THE FULLEST EXTENT PERMITTED BY LAW, CONTRACTOR'S TOTAL LIABILITY TO THE OWNER FOR ANY AND ALL INJURIES, CLAIMS, LOSSES, EXPENSES, AND/OR DAMAGES ARISING OUT OF THIS OR RELATING TO THIS AGREEMENT FROM ANY CAUSE OR CAUSES, SHALL NOT EXCEED THE ACTUAL AMOUNT PAID BY OWNER, SUCH CAUSES INCLUDE, BUT ARE NOT LIMITED TO, CONTRACTOR'S NEGLIGENCE, ERRORS, OMISSIONS, STRICT LIABILITY, FRAUD, BREACH OF CONTRACT, AND/OR BREACH OF WARRANTY, WHETHER EXPRESS OR IMPLIED.

DISPUTE RESOLUTION: The Owner and Contractor agree that all claims, disputes or controversies arising out of or in relation to the interpretation, application, or enforcement of services provided under this contract shall first be attempted to be decided through non-binding (formal) mediation, with costs shared equally between the parties. If this process fails then the two parties must enter into binding arbitration to be administered and conducted by The McCammon Group according to its standard arbitration rules governing at the time one of the parties initiates a claim. In the event Contractor is the prevailing party in any litigation or arbitration arising out of or relating to this Agreement, Contractor shall be entitled to recover all reasonable attorney's fees, costs and expenses of litigation, expert fees, including all filing, administrative and arbitration fees. DUE TO THE SPECIALIZED NATURE OF CONSTRUCTION DISPUTES, EACH PARTY HEREBY WAIVES ITS RIGHT TO A TRIAL BY JURY.

TIME BAR TO LEGAL ACTION: The Owner and Contractor agree that claims from either party, including any assigned claims, for breach of this contract or for alleged failure to perform in accordance with the Standard of Care shall not be initiated more than one (1) year from the date of Substantial Completion.

THIRD PARTY BENEFICIARY: The Owner and Contractor agree that the services performed by Contractor pursuant to this contract are solely for the benefit of the Owner and are not intended by either the Owner or Contractor to benefit any other person or entity.

APPLICABLE LAW: This agreement between the Owner and Contractor shall be governed by the laws of the jurisdiction in which the project is located, and shall not be assigned without written consent. If any part of this contract is found to be unenforceable, that part shall be considered modified appropriately to conform to the law; all other terms of this contract shall continue to be in force and legally binding.

ENTIRE AGREEMENT: This agreement represents the entire agreement between the Owner and Contractor and supersedes any prior negotiations, representations, or agreements. This agreement may be amended only by written instrument signed by both the Owner and Contractor.

SEEN AND AGREED this _____ day of _____, 2007

_____   _____
Construction Company   Owner

                                         _____
                                         Date

APPENDIX I

NAME OF COMPANY

THIS AGREEMENT, Made as of _____, in the Year of _____.

Between the Owner:

And the Contractor: NAME OF COMPANY
Bus. License
State License

For the Project:

The Architect for
The Project is: _____
_____
_____

The Owner and Contractor agree as set forth below (the "Agreement"):

ARTICLE I - GENERAL PROVISIONS

1.1 Basic Definitions.

    1.1.1. The Contract Documents consist of this Agreement, the approved Construction Documents (as defined in Article 14), any and all Modifications, and any and all Change Orders (as defined in Section 8.1.1 below). A Modification is a written amendment to this Agreement signed by both parties. These documents form the Contract, and are as fully a part of the Contract as if attached to this Agreement or set forth herein.

    1.1.2. The Project is the construction for which Contractor is responsible under this Agreement, as set forth in the Contract Documents, and all labor, materials, and equipment used or incorporated in such construction.

    1.1.3. The Work comprises the completed construction designed under the Project, and includes labor necessary to produce such construction, and the materials and equipment incorporated in such construction.

1.2 Execution, Correlation, and Intent.

    1.2.1. This Agreement shall be executed in duplicate by the Owner and the Contractor.

1.2.2. It is the intent of the parties that the Contract Documents include all items necessary for proper execution and completion of the Work. The Contract Documents are complimentary, and what is required by any one shall be as binding as if required by all. Words and abbreviations that have well known technical or trade meanings are used in the Contract Documents in accordance with such recognized meanings. The Construction Documents are listed in Article 14.

1.3   Ownership and Use of the Documents.

1.3.1 The drawings, specifications and other documents furnished by Contractor are instruments of service and shall not become the property of the Owner whether or not the Project for which they are made is commenced. Drawings, Specifications and other documents furnished by the Contractor shall not be used by the Owner for other projects, for additions to this Project, or, unless Contractor is in default under this Agreement, for completion of this Project by others, except by written agreement relating to use, liability, and compensation.

1.3.2 Submission or distribution of documents to meet official regulatory requirements or for other purposes in connection with the Project is not to be construed as publication in derogation of Contractor's common law copyrights or other reserved rights. The Owner shall own neither the documents nor the copyrights.

ARTICLE 2 - CONTRACTOR RESPONSIBILITIES

2.1   Services and Responsibilities.

2.1.1. Contractor shall be responsible for the performance of its subcontractors and subconsultants. Nothing contained in this Agreement shall create any professional obligation or contractual relationship between such persons or entities and the Owner. Construction services shall be performed by qualified construction subcontractors and suppliers selected and paid by Contractor.

2.2   Basic Services.

2.2.1. Contractor's Basic Services are described below and in Article 14 of this Agreement.

2.2.2. Contractor shall prepare applications for and obtain all required building permits. The Contractor shall pay the fees for the Building Permit unless the Contract Documents specify otherwise, with such costs to be a portion of the compensation set forth in Article 5 below.

2.2.3. Contractor shall be responsible for all means, methods, techniques, sequences, and procedures.

2.2.4. Contractor shall keep the Owner reasonably informed of the progress of the Work.

2.2.5. <u>Warranty.</u>

2.2.5.1. Contractor warrants to the Owner that materials and equipment incorporated in the Work will be new unless otherwise specified, and that the Work will be of good quality, free from faults and defects, and in reasonable conformance with the Contract Documents and applicable building code requirements. This warranty is effective for a period of one year from substantial completion as defined herein. Notice of defects must be received within the warranty period or all such claims are waived. Work not conforming to these requirements shall be corrected according to Article 9.

2.2.5.2. The Contractor's warranty excludes remedy for damage or defect caused by abuse, modifications not executed by the Contractor, improper or insufficient maintenance, improper operation or normal wear and tear or usage.

2.2.6. Contractor shall keep the premises reasonably free from accumulation of waste materials or rubbish caused by Contractor's operations. At the completion of the Work, Contractor shall remove from and about the premises Contractor's tools, construction equipment, machinery, surplus materials, waste materials, and rubbish.

2.2.7. Contractor shall: (i) prepare Change Orders requested for the Owner's approval and execution, and (ii) shall have authority to make minor changes in the construction consistent with the intent of the Contract Documents not involving an adjustment in the contract sum or an extension of the contract time.

2.2.8. In the event that Contractor encounters on the site material reasonably believed to be hazardous, which has not been rendered harmless, Contractor shall immediately stop work in the affected area and report the condition to the Owner in writing. The Work shall not be resumed until the hazardous material is rendered harmless and both the Owner and Contractor agree in writing to continue the Work. Unless the Work under this Agreement includes the specific handling, disturbance, removal, or transportation of hazardous materials, waste, or asbestos, upon discovery of such hazardous materials the Contractor shall notify the Owner immediately and allow the Contractor to contract with a properly licensed and qualified hazardous materials contractor. Any such work shall be treated as a Change Order resulting in additional costs and time considerations.

2.2.9. When possible, Contractor shall maintain at the site for the Owner, one record copy of the approved Construction Documents, in good order and marked currently to record changes in selections made during construction.

ARTICLE 3 - THE OWNER

3.1. The Owner shall designate a representative authorized to act on the Owner's behalf with respect to the Project. The Owner or such authorized representative shall examine documents submitted by Contractor and shall, within 24 hours, render written decisions pertaining thereto to avoid delay in the orderly progress of the Work. All directives, requests for information and changes in the Work shall be in writing.

3.2. The Owner shall furnish services by land surveyors, geotechnical engineers and other consultants for subsoil, air and water conditions, and when such services reasonably are deemed necessary by Contractor to properly carry out the Work.

3.3. The Owner shall furnish structural, mechanical, chemical, geotechnical, and their laboratory or on site tests, inspections, and reports, as required by law or the Contract Documents.

3.4. The Owner shall furnish the drawings and specifications set forth in Article 14. The Contractor shall be entitled to rely upon the accuracy and completeness of the documents set forth in Article 14.

3.5. The services, information, surveys, reports, tests and drawings and specifications required by paragraphs 3.2, 3.3, and 3.4 shall be furnished at the Owner's expense, and Contractor shall be entitled to reply upon their accuracy and completeness.

3.6. If the Owner observes or otherwise becomes aware of a fault or defect in the Work or non-conformity with the Construction Documents, the Owner shall give prompt written notice to the Contractor.

3.7. The Owner shall furnish the required information and services and shall promptly render decisions pertaining thereto to avoid delay in the orderly progress of the Work.

3.8. Contractor shall assign a Project Manager to the Project. The Owner shall communicate with the Contractor only through the Project Manager. Contractor will not be responsible for any work that is not authorized or directed
through the Project Manager.

3.9. The Owner shall communicate with subcontractors **ONLY** through the Contractor. The Owner shall not give instructions or orders to employees or workmen of Contractor or to any subcontractor or subcontractor's employees. The Owner will be responsible for any part of the Work, and any resulting delays or increased costs to the Work, which is not directed in writing through the Contractor's Project Manager.

3.10. The Owner shall not engage or otherwise hire any employee or subcontractor of Contractor to perform any work until final payment (as defined in Article 5.2) is received. Violation of this clause shall be considered cause for immediate termination for cause by the Contractor as set forth below.

3.11. The Owner shall not engage or otherwise hire any workman or subcontractor to work for Owner to perform any work on the Project until final payment (as defined in Article 5.2) is received. Violation of this clause shall be considered cause for immediate termination for cause by the Contractor as set forth below.

3.12. If the Owner chooses to supply materials to be incorporated into the Work, the Owner will be responsible for the inspection, coordination and warranty of those materials unless otherwise agreed to in writing. If the Contractor is requested to purchase material that the Owner was going to provide, the Contractor's time and cost shall be appropriately adjusted by Change Order.

ARTICLE 4 - TIME

4.1. Contractor shall provide services as expeditiously as is consistent with reasonable skill and care in the orderly progress of the Work.

4.2. If Contractor is delayed in the progress of the Project by acts or neglect of the Owner, or its agents, changes order in the Work not caused by the fault of the Contractor, labor disputes, fire, unusual delay in transportation, adverse weather, unavoidable casualties, or other causes beyond the Contractor's control, or another cause that the Owner and Contractor agree is justifiable, the Contract Time and Contract Sum shall be adjusted appropriately by Change Order.

4.3. <u>Date of Commencement and Substantial Completion.</u>

4.3.1. The date of commencement shall be determined at the sole discretion of the Contractor after receipt by the Contractor of all of the following (the "Commencement Date"):

(a) Initial cash payments, if any, called for in any draw schedule established by the parties and attached hereto;

(b) Evidence satisfactory to Contractor of Owner's ability to complete payment of all sums set forth in this Agreement including, but not limited to, a letter of commitment from a lending institution acceptable to Contractor, certified bank records evidencing funds necessary to complete payment under the terms of this Agreement or other documents as reasonably required by Contractor in order to assess Owner's financial capability;

(c) Written approval of plans and specifications by the controlling architectural review committee(s), if any; and

(d) All necessary governmental approvals and permits, if any.

4.3.2. In the event the Owner does not provide Contractor all of the above listed items in a timely fashion after execution of this Agreement, or for reasons beyond Contractor's control the Property cannot be developed in accordance with this Agreement, or Owner cannot perform his payment or other obligations under this Agreement within a reasonable time after execution of this Agreement, Contractor may, in its sole discretion, cancel this Agreement, and return to Owner any monies paid on deposit deducting therefrom any and all expenses, administrative or otherwise, incurred by the Contractor, but in no event shall such expenses be less than $5,000.00, and all parties shall be relieved of any further liability or obligations hereunder. This provision shall not act as a waiver by Contractor of other legal or equitable remedies for breach of contract or a default by Owner.

4.3.3. The Contractor estimates that substantial completion of the entire Work shall occur within _____ days from the Commencement Date (the "Date of Substantial Completion"). The Date of Substantial Completion of the Work is the date when the construction is sufficiently complete, according to the Contract Documents, so that the Owner can occupy or use the Work for the use for which it is intended, as contemplated by the Contract Documents. If Contractor shall be delayed at any time in the progress of construction by Acts of God, labor disputes, Contractor's inability to obtain material and/or labor, inclement weather, acts of default, and/or negligence or interference on the part of the Owner, and any other causes beyond the control of the Contractor, in such event the substantial completion date shall be extended for twice the number of days equal to the period of such delay. In no event shall such delay constitute abandonment by Contractor and the delays caused by such events shall not be included in calculating time frames for payment or performance. The Contractor shall not be liable for loss(es) and/or damage(s) resulting directly or indirectly from any delays in the completion of construction.

ARTICLE 5 - PAYMENT

5.1. Contract Sum, Progress Payments and Final Payment.

5.1.1. The Owner shall pay the Contractor for the Contractor's performance of this Agreement, the initial Contract Sum of zero thousands, zero hundreds and zero ($00,000.00) (the "Contract Sum").

5.1.2. Payment Schedule.

Initial Deposit =	$ upon signing this Contract
Second Draw =	$ upon commencement of Construction
Third Draw =	$ Framing completed
Fourth Draw =	$ Windows substantially set
Fifth Draw =	$ commencement of plumbing rough-ins
Six Draw =	$ commencement of electrical rough-ins
Seventh Draw =	$ concealment inspection

Eighth Draw =	$ Sheetrock is hung
Ninth Draw =	$ tile is installed
Tenth Draw =	$ hardwood floor is installed
Eleventh Draw =	$ final inspection
Final Payment =	$ completion of punch list

5.1.3. Invoices will be submitted based on the Payment Schedule in Article 5.1.2.

5.1.4. Payment is due in full upon presentation of a properly submitted invoice for payment. Should payment not be made within ten (10) days of the invoice, interest shall accrue from the date of the invoice at the rate specified in Article 12.3.

5.1.5. Where the price of material, equipment, or labor increases significantly during the term of the contract through no fault of the Contractor, the Contract Sum shall be equitably adjusted by Change Order as provided for in Article 8 of this Agreement. A significant price increase means a change in price from the date of the contract execution during the first four months of the contract by an amount exceeding ten-percent (10%). Such price increases shall be documented by vendor quotes, invoices, catalogs, receipts or other documents of commercial use. Where the delivery of materials is delayed through no fault of the Contractor, the Owner shall not hold the Contractor liable for costs associated with such delay.

5.1.6. The Owner shall have no obligation to pay or otherwise be responsible in any way to any subcontractor except as may otherwise be required by law.

5.1.7. Contractor warrants that: (1) title to the Work covered by an invoice for payment will pass to the Owner either by incorporation in construction or upon receipt of payment by Contractor, whichever occurs first; and (2) Work covered by paid invoices for payment is free and clear of all liens.

5.1.8. Contractor shall notify the Owner when the Work or an agreed upon portion thereof is substantially completed by issuing a Certificate of Substantial Completion that shall establish the Date of Substantial Completion. Following receipt of the Certificate of Substantial Completion, the Owner may also prepare and deliver to Contractor a list of items to be completed or corrected. The Owner and Contractor shall review the respective lists and inspect the Work together and shall agree upon a consolidated list of items to be completed or corrected (the Punch List). Contractor will provide the Owner in writing a time of completion and value for each item on the Punch List.

5.1.9. The Punch List agreed to by the Owner and the Contractor will be the only and final Punch List.

5.2. <u>Final Payment.</u>

5.2.1. Final payment, constituting the entire unpaid balance due, shall be paid by the Owner to Contractor upon the Owner's receipt of Contractor's final invoice for payment after the Work described in the Punch List is completed and this Agreement has been fully performed, except for those responsibilities of the Contractor which survive this Agreement.

5.2.2. The making of final payment shall constitute a waiver of all claims by the Owner against the Contractor except for properly preserved warranty claims which may survive this Agreement.

5.2.3. Acceptance of final payment shall constitute a waiver of all claims by Contractor against the Owner, except those previously made in writing and identified by Contractor as unsettled at the time of the submission of the final invoice for payment.

ARTICLE 6 - PROTECTION OF PERSONS AND PROPERTY

6.1. Contractor shall be responsible for initiating, maintaining, and providing supervision of safety precautions and programs in connection with the Work.

6.2. Contractor shall take reasonable precautions for safety of and shall provide reasonable protection to prevent damage, injury, or loss to: 1) employees on the Work and other persons who may be affected thereby; 2) the Work and materials and equipment to be incorporated therein; and 3) other persons and property at or adjacent to the site.

6.3. Contractor shall give notices and comply with applicable laws, ordinances, rules, regulations and orders of public authorities bearing on the safety of persons and property and their protection from damage, injury or loss.

6.4. Contractor shall be liable for damage or loss, but only to the extent permitted under this Agreement, (other than damage or loss to property insured under the property insurance provided or required by the Contract Documents to be provided by the Owner) to property at the site caused in whole or in part by Contractor, a subcontractor of Contractor, or anyone directly or indirectly employed be either of them, except damage or loss attributable to the acts or omissions of the Owner, the Owner's separate contractors or anyone directly or indirectly employed by them or by anyone for whose acts they may be liable and not attributable to the fault or negligence of Contractor.

ARTICLE 7 - INSURANCE AND BONDS

7.1. <u>Contractor's Liability Insurance.</u>

7.1.1. Contractor shall purchase and maintain in a company or companies authorized to do business in the state in which the Work is located such insurance as will protect Contractor from claims set forth below which may arise out of or result from operations under the Contract by Contractor or by a subcontractor of Contractor, or by anyone directly or indirectly employed by any of them, or by anyone for whose acts they may be liable:

7.1.1.1. Claims under worker's or workmen's compensation, disability benefit and other similar employee benefit laws which are applicable to the Work to be performed;

7.1.1.2. Claims for damages because of bodily injury, occupational sickness or disease, or death of Contractor's employees under any applicable employer liability law;

7.1.1.3. Claims covered by Contractor's General Liability policy.

7.2 Owner's Liability Insurance.

7.2.1. The Owner shall be responsible for purchasing and maintaining, in a company or companies authorized to do business in the state in which the principal improvements are to be located, Owner's liability insurance to protect the Owner against claims that may arise from operations under this Project. The Owner shall notify Contractor, within ten days, of cancellation or change in such policy.

7.3. Owner's Property Insurance.

7.3.1. Unless otherwise provided under this Agreement, the Owner shall purchase and maintain, in a company or companies authorized to do business in the state in which the principal improvements are to be located, property insurance upon the Work to the full insurance value thereof. It shall insure against perils of fire and extended coverage and shall include all risk insurance for physical loss or damage including, without duplication of coverage, theft, vandalism, and malicious mischief. If Contractor is damaged by failure of the Owner to purchase or maintain such insurance without notice to Contractor, then the Owner shall bear all reasonable costs properly attributable thereto.

7.3.2. The Owner and Contractor waive all rights against each other and the contractors, subcontractors, agents and employees, each of the other, for damages caused by fire or other perils to the extent covered by property or liability insurance obtained, or required to be obtained, or other insurance applicable to the Work, except that such rights as they may have to proceeds of such insurance held by the Owner as trustee.

7.4. Loss of Use Insurance.

7.4.1. The Owner, at the Owner's option, may purchase and maintain such insurance as will insure the Owner against loss of use of the Owner's property due to fire, other hazards, or any other cause. The Owner waives all rights of action against Contractor, and its subcontractors and their agents, employees, for loss of use of the Owner's property, including, but not limited to, consequential losses.

ARTICLE 8 - CHANGES IN THE WORK

8.1. Change Orders.

8.1.1. A Change Order is a written order signed by both the Owner and Contractor, and issued after the execution of this Agreement, authorizing a change in the Work or adjustments in the contract sum or contract time. The Work, the Contract Sum and Contract Time may be changed only by Change Order.

8.1.2. The Owner, without invalidating this Agreement, may order changes in the Work within the general scope of this Agreement consisting of additions, deletions, or other revisions, and the contract sum and contract time shall be adjusted accordingly. Such changes in the Work shall be authorized by Change Order, and shall be performed under applicable conditions of the Contract Documents. If Contractor performs the Work as requested by the Owner, and Owner refuses to sign the Change Order, Owner agrees Contractor shall be entitled to payment for such Work the same as if the proposed Change Order had actually been executed.

8.1.3. If the Owner requests a change in the Work, and then elects not to proceed with the change, a Change Order shall be issued to reimburse Contractor for any costs incurred. Costs include, but shall not be limited to, analysis and research into the requested change in the Work. The minimum cost will be $150 to cover administrative time and research associated with the proposed Change Order.

8.1.4. A $150 administrative fee will be charged for processing each Change Order. This fee will not be charged for adjustment of allowance items or change of time or (unit price items.)

8.1.5. Cost or credit to the Owner resulting from a change in the Work shall be determined in one or more of the following ways:

8.1.5.1. by mutual acceptance of a lump sum properly itemized;

8.1.5.2. by unit prices or allowances stated in the Contract Documents or subsequently agreed upon;

8.1.5.3. by time and materials cost itemized and supported by time records and material invoices plus 15% overhead and 15% profit.

The parties agree to decide on one of the above methods prior to commencing work and shall cross through the other two methods

8.2. Concealed Conditions.

8.2.1. Should concealed conditions be encountered in the performance of the Work below the surface of the ground, or concealed or unknown conditions in an existing structure at variance with the conditions indicated by the Contract Documents, the Contract Sum and Contract Time shall be equitably adjusted by Change Order upon claim by either party made within seven days after the first observation of the condition.

8.3. Regulatory Changes.

8.3.1 Contractor shall be compensated for changes in the Work required by the enactment, revision, or interpretation of codes, laws or regulations subsequent to the submission of Contractor's Proposal.

ARTICLE 9 - CORRECTION OF WORK

9.1 Contractor shall correct Work under this Agreement found to be defective or nonconforming within a period of one year from the date of Substantial Completion. Owner shall comply with notice requirements of warranty claims in accordance with 2.2.5.1 herein.

ARTICLE 10 - CLAIMS AND LIMITATION OF LIABILITY

10.1. Claims for Damages.

10.1.1. Should either party to this Agreement suffer injury or damage of any kind because of an act or omission of the other party, the other party's employees or agents, or another for whose acts the other party is legally responsible, claims shall be made within seven (7) days after such injury or damage is or should be first discovered. If no claim is made within this time frame, then it is forever waived and barred.

10.1.2. Contractor shall review and inspect the Work with the Owner:

10.1.2.1. At concealment;
10.1.2.2. At completion of prime painting;
10.1.2.3. At substantial completion.

At each inspection, Contractor and the Owner will complete checklists showing the Contractor's Work is in substantial compliance with the Contract Documents.

10.2 LIMITATION OF LIABILITY AND REMEDIES: IN RECOGNITION OF THE RELATIVE RISKS, REWARDS, AND BENEFITS OF THE PROJECT TO BOTH THE OWNER AND CONTRACTOR, THE RISKS HAVE BEEN ALLOCATED SUCH THAT THE OWNER AGREES THAT, TO THE FULLEST EXTENT PERMITTED BY LAW, CONTRACTOR'S TOTAL LIABILITY TO THE OWNER FOR ANY AND ALL INJURIES, CLAIMS, LOSSES, EXPENSES, AND/OR DAMAGES ARISING OUT OF OR RELATING TO THIS AGREEMENT FROM ANY CAUSE OR CAUSES, SHALL NOT EXCEED THE ACTUAL AMOUNT PAID, SUCH CAUSES INCLUDE, BUT ARE NOT LIMITED TO, CONTRACTOR'S NEGLIGENCE, ERRORS, OMISSIONS, STRICT LIABILITY, FRAUD, BREACH OF CONTRACT, AND/OR BREACH OF WARRANTY, WHETHER EXPRESS OR IMPLIED. UNDER NO CIRCUMSTANCES SHALL CONTRACTOR BE LIABLE FOR ANY SPECIAL, INDIRECT OR CONSEQUENTIAL DAMAGES, INCLUDING, WITHOUT LIMITATION, ANY DAMAGES BASED ON A CLAIM OF DIMINUTION

IN THE VALUE OF THE HOME OR LOSS OF BARGAIN. NO ACTION, REGARDLESS OF FORM, INCLUDING ARBITRATION, ARISING OUT OF OR RELATING TO THIS CONTRACT MAY BE BROUGHT BY OWNER MORE THAN ONE YEAR AFTER THE CAUSE OF ACTION HAS ACCRUED. MOREOVER, CONTRACTOR EXPRESSLY DISCLAIMS LIABILITY, AND OWNER EXPRESSLY WAIVES ANY AND ALL CLAIMS FOR PROPERTY AND/OR PERSONAL INJURY OR OTHER ECONOMIC LOSS RESULTING FROM ENVIRONMENTAL CONDITIONS, INCLUDING, BUT NOT LIMITED TO, RADON GAS, ASBESTOS, MOLD AND FORMALDEHYDE.

ARTICLE 11 - DEFAULT AND TERMINATION OF THE AGREEMENT

11.1. <u>Owner's Defaults.</u>

11.1.1. Contractor shall have the right to stop all Work on the Project and keep the job idle if payments are not timely made to Contractor, or if Owner repeatedly fails or refuses to furnish Contractor with access to the job site and/or product selections or information necessary for the advancement of Contractor's Work. Simultaneous with stopping work on the Project the Contractor will provide the Owner with written notice of the nature of Owner's default and shall give the Owner a 14-day period in which to cure this default.

11.1.2. If Work is stopped due to any of the above reasons (or for any other breach of contract by Owner) for a period of 14 days and the Owner has failed to take significant steps to cure such default or defaults, then Contractor may, without prejudicing any other remedies Contractor may have, give written notice of termination of the Contract to Owner and demand payment for all completed work and materials ordered through the date of work stoppage and any other loss or damage sustained by Contractor, including Contractor's Profit and Overhead at the rate of 25% on the balance of the incomplete Work under the Contract and for proven losses sustained upon materials, equipment, tools, and construction equipment and machinery, and labor, including overhead and profit and damages. Thereafter, Contractor shall be relieved from all other contractual duties and obligations, including, but not limited to, all Punch List and warranty work, if any. At such time all such warranties hereunder shall be deemed null and void.

11.2. <u>Contractor's Defaults.</u>

11.2.1. If Contractor defaults or persistently fails or neglects to carry out the Work accordingly to the Contract Documents or fails to substantially perform the provisions of the Agreement, the Owner, upon certification of an architect registered in the (state of) may give written notice that the Owner intends to terminate this Agreement. If Contractor fails to begin to correct the defaults within 14 days after being given notice, the Owner shall then give a second written notice and, after an additional 14 days, the Owner may without prejudice to any other remedy, make good such deficiencies and may deduct the cost thereof from the payment due Contractor. If the unpaid balance of the contract sum exceeds the expense of finishing the Work, the excess shall be paid to Contractor, but if the expense exceeds the unpaid balance, Contractor shall pay the difference to the Owner.

ARTICLE 12 - BASIS OF COMPENSATION

12.1. The Owner shall compensate the Contractor according to Article 5 and other provisions of this Agreement.

_____
_____
_____

12.2. Interest.

12.3.1. Interest on balances of invoices unpaid within ten (10) days of the invoice shall accrue at the rate of 1.5% per month, 18% per annum, from the date of the invoice on all outstanding balances.

ARTICLE 13 - MISCELLANEOUS PROVISIONS

13.1. This Agreement shall be governed in all respects by the laws of the **SPECIFC STATE.**

13.2. This Agreement is the result of negotiation between the parties each of whom had the right to be represented by counsel. In the event of any ambiguities, such ambiguities shall not be construed in favor of or against any party irrespective of which party acted as scrivener and irrespective of any statutory or evidentiary rule of contract interpretation or construction to the contrary.

3.3. The Owner waives all rights against Contractor and any of its subcontractors, agents and employees, for damages caused by fire or other causes of loss to the extent covered by property insurance obtained by Owner, or other property insurance applicable to the Work. A waiver of subrogation shall be effective as to a person or entity even though that person or entity would otherwise have a duty of indemnification, contractual or otherwise, did not pay the insurance premium directly or indirectly, and whether or not the person or entity had an insurable interest in the property damaged.

13.4. The Owner and Contractor agree that all claims, disputes or controversies arising out of or in relation to the interpretation, application, or enforcement of services provided under this Agreement, including allegations of fraud, misrepresentation or violation of any state or federal laws or regulations, arising under, as a result of, or in connection with this Agreement, the Work performed by Contractor, and/or the parties' relationship, shall first be attempted to be decided by mediation before resorting to arbitration, litigation, or some other dispute resolution procedure. The parties agree to use The McCammon Group and to convene the mediation at the offices of the Contractor, or at a mutually agreed location. The fees for the mediation will be borne equally by the parties. If the dispute cannot be resolved by mediation, the parties agree to arbitrate the dispute.

The arbitration will be administered and conducted by The McCammon Group according to its standard arbitration rules governing at the time one of the parties initiates a claim. The fees for the arbitration services shall be borne equally by the parties in the first instance. In the event Contractor is the prevailing party in any litigation or arbitration arising out of or relating to this Agreement, Contractor shall be entitled to recover all reasonable attorney's fees, costs and expenses of litigation, expert fees, including all filing, administrative and arbitration fees.

13.5. In the case of default of payment by the Owner, the Owner agrees to pay any and all reasonably reasonable collection fees, including internal costs, internal time, reasonable attorney's fees, court costs, and other costs incurred by Contractor.

13.6. The headings of articles and paragraphs are for convenience only and shall not modify the rights and obligations created by this Agreement.

13.7. In case any provision of this Agreement is held to be illegal, invalid, or unenforceable, the validity, legality and enforceability of the remaining provisions shall not be affected.

13.8. WAIVER OF TRIAL BY JURY: THE OWNER AND CONTRACTOR FOR THEMSELVES, THEIR HEIRS, SUCCESSORS AND ASSIGNS, VOLUNTARILY AND KNOWINGLY WAIVE THEIR RIGHT TO TRIAL BY JURY OF ANY AND ALL ISSUES RELATING TO THIS TRANSACTION INCLUDING BUT NOT LIMITED TO ANY ISSUES RELATED TO THIS CONTRACT, THE SETTLEMENT, THE WARRANTYS, OR THE CONVEYANCE OF THE PROPERTY.

13.9. OTHER EXCLUSIONS: THE PARTIES HERETO ACKNOWLEDGE THAT THIS CONTRACT IS NOT FOR THE SALE OF GOODS AND SERVICES BUT IS STRICTLY AND SOLELY FOR THE CONSTRUCTION OF IMPROVEMENTS TO REAL ESTATE AND THAT NO ACTION MAY BE BROUGHT OR MAINTAINED AGAINST CONTRACTOR FOR VIOLATION OF THE VIRGINIA CONSUMER PROTECTION ACT AS ENACTED IN VIRGINIA. TO THE EXTENT PERMITTED BY LAW, THE OWNER WAIVES ANY RIGHTS IT MIGHT HAVE UNDER THE VIRGINIA CONSUMER PROTECTION ACT, IF ANY.

13.10. This Agreement shall be binding on successors, assigns, and legal representatives of the Owner and Contractor. Neither party shall assign, sublet, or transfer an interest in this Agreement without the written consent of the other.

13.11. This Agreement represents the entire agreement between the Owner and Contractor and supersedes any prior negotiations, representations, or agreements. This Agreement may be amended only by written instrument signed by both the Owner and Contractor.

13.12. Except as expressly provided herein, the parties mutually waive all claims against each other for consequential damages arising out of or relating to the Project.

13.13. All claims arising out of or relating to the Project or this Agreement shall accrue not later than the date of Substantial Completion of the Project as defined above.

13.14. Time shall be of the essence with respect to all of the Owner's obligations hereunder.

13.15. In the event of a default by Owner, the Contractor shall be entitled to its costs and attorney's fees provided that Contractor is the prevailing party in any litigation.

13.16. Whenever by the terms of this Agreement any notices are required to be given, notice shall be conclusively given when deposited in the United States mail via certified mail with return receipt requested, postage prepaid, to any of the parties at the addresses set out herein, or by telecopy provided that the party sending the telecopy provides a receipt showing receipt by the other party, or by commercial carrier such as UPS or Fed Ex provided a receipt is provided showing receipt by the party being provided the notice:

To Contractor: NAME OF COMPANY
CONTRACTOR NAME
ADDRESS

To Owner(s): _____ P:_____
_____ F:_____
_____
_____

ARTICLE 14 - CONSTRUCTION DOCUMENTS

14.1. The drawings and specifications are hereby enumerated as follows:
Appendix
Appendix
Appendix

SEEN AND AGREED:

_____   _____
NAME OF COMPANY   Date
Principal

_____   _____
(Owner)   Date

_____   _____
(Owner)

APPENDIX J

CHANGE ORDER

Change Order No.:_____   Contract No._____

To: _____   Date:_____
        _____
        _____

Project Name_____

Under our AGREEMENT dated _____, _____ (Year)

You hereby are authorized and directed to make the following change(s) in accordance with terms and conditions of the Agreement:

(DESCRIPTION OF THE CHANGE)

FOR THE Additive (Deductive) Sum of: _____($ _____).

Original Agreement Amount	$_____
Sum of Previous Changes	$_____
This Change Order Add (Deduct)	$_____
Present Agreement Amount	$_____

The time for completion shall be (increased/decreased) by _____(____) calendar days due to this Change Order. Accordingly, the Contract Time is now _____(____) calendar days and the substantial completion date is _____. Your acceptance of this Change Order shall constitute a modification to our Agreement and will be performed subject to all the same terms and conditions in our Agreement indicated above, as fully as if the same were repeated in this acceptance.

The adjustment, if any, to this Agreement shall constitute a full and final settlement of any and all claims arising out of or related to the change set forth herein, including claims for impact and delay costs.

The Contract Administrator has directed the Contractor to increase the penal sum of the existing Performance and Payment Bonds or to obtain additional bonds on the basis of a $25,000.00 or greater value change order.
9 Check if applicable and provide written confirmation from the bonding company/agent (attorney-in-fact) that the amount of the Performance and Payment Bonds have been adjusted to 100% of the new contract amount.

Accepted _____, _____(Year)

By:_____   By:_____
              Contractor   Architect/Engineer

By:_____
              Owner

APPENDIX K

CERTIFICATE OF LIABILITY INSURANCE

OP ID EE SSELE-1

DATE (MM/DD/YYYY)

PRODUCT

THIS CERTIFICATE IS ISSUED AS A MATTER OF INFORMATION ONLY AND CONFERS NO RIGHTS UPON THE CERTIFICATE HOLDER. THIS CERTIFICATE DOES NOT AMEND, EXTEND OR ALTER THE COVERAGE AFFORDED BY THE POLICIES BELOW.

INSURED

INSURERS AFFORDING COVERAGE	NAIC #
INSURER A:	
INSURER B:	
INSURER C:	
INSURER D:	
INSURER E:	

COVERAGES

THE POLICIES OF INSURANCE LISTED BELOW HAVE BEEN ISSUED TO THE INSURED NAMED ABOVE FOR THE POLICY PERIOD INDICATED. NOTWITHSTANDING ANY REQUIREMENT, TERM OR CONDITION OF ANY CONTRACT OR OTHER DOCUMENT WITH RESPECT TO WHICH THIS CERTIFICATE MAY BE ISSUED OR MAY PERTAIN, THE INSURANCE AFFORDED BY THE POLICIES DESCRIBED HEREIN IS SUBJECT TO ALL THE TERMS, EXCLUSIONS AND CONDITIONS OF SUCH POLICIES. AGGREGATE LIMITS SHOWN MAY HAVE BEEN REDUCED BY PAID CLAIMS.

INSR LTR	ADD'L INSRD	TYPE OF INSURANCE	POLICY NUMBER	POLICY EFFECTIVE DATE (MM/DD/YYYY)	POLICY EXPIRATION DATE (MM/DD/YYYY)	LIMITS	
A		**GENERAL LIABILITY** [X] COMMERCIAL GENERAL LIABILITY [ ] CLAIMS MADE [X] OCCUR				EACH OCCURRENCE	$1000000
						DAMAGE TO RENTED PREMISES (Ea occurrence)	$500000
						MED EXP (Any one person)	$10000
						PERSONAL & ADV INJURY	$1000000
						GENERAL AGGREGATE	$2000000
		GEN'L AGGREGATE LIMIT APPLIES PER: [ ] POLICY [ ] PROJECT [ ] LOC				PRODUCTS - COMP/OP AGG	$2000000
		AUTOMOBILE LIABILITY [ ] ANY AUTO [ ] ALL OWNED AUTOS [ ] SCHEDULED AUTOS [ ] HIRED AUTOS [ ] NON-OWNED AUTOS				COMBINED SINGLE LIMIT (Ea accident)	$
						BODILY INJURY (Per person)	$
						BODILY INJURY (Per accident)	$
						PROPERTY DAMAGE (Per accident)	$
		GARAGE LIABILITY [ ] ANY AUTO				AUTO ONLY - EA ACCIDENT	$
						OTHER THAN AUTO ONLY: EA ACC	$
						AGG	$
		EXCESS / UMBRELLA LIABILITY [ ] OCCUR [ ] CLAIMS MADE				EACH OCCURRENCE	$
						AGGREGATE	$
							$
		[ ] DEDUCTIBLE [ ] RETENTION $					$
							$
A		**WORKERS COMPENSATION AND EMPLOYERS' LIABILITY** ANY PROPRIETOR/PARTNER/EXECUTIVE OFFICER/MEMBER EXCLUDED? Y/N (Mandatory in NH) If yes, describe under SPECIAL PROVISIONS below				WC STATU-TORY LIMITS / OTH-ER	
						E.L. EACH ACCIDENT	$100000
						E.L. DISEASE - EA EMPLOYEE	$100000
						E.L. DISEASE - POLICY LIMIT	$500000
		OTHER					

DESCRIPTION OF OPERATIONS / LOCATIONS / VEHICLES / EXCLUSIONS ADDED BY ENDORSEMENT / SPECIAL PROVISIONS

CERTIFICATE HOLDER

CANCELLATION

SHOULD ANY OF THE ABOVE DESCRIBED POLICIES BE CANCELLED BEFORE THE EXPIRATION DATE THEREOF, THE ISSUING INSURER WILL ENDEAVOR TO MAIL _____ DAYS WRITTEN NOTICE TO THE CERTIFICATE HOLDER NAMED TO THE LEFT, BUT FAILURE TO DO SO SHALL IMPOSE NO OBLIGATION OR LIABILITY OF ANY KIND UPON THE INSURER, ITS AGENTS OR REPRESENTATIVES.

AUTHORIZED REPRESENTATIVE
Donna McGhee

ACORD 25 (2009/01) © 1988-2009 ACORD CORPORATION. All rights reserved.
The ACORD name and logo are registered marks of ACORD

APPENDIX L

The following finishing level definitions are summations for industry standards. The official guidelines can be found online.

Level 1 one might find this in attics, crawl spaces or areas that are generally concealed. All joints are taped with joint compound. Tape and fastener heads are not covered with joint compound. Surfaces are free of excess joint compound but some tool marks are normal. This provides a degree of sound and smoke control.

Level 2 generally used in areas where water-resistant gypsum or cement backing board is used as a substrate for tile. I suggest fiberglass tape be used due to moisture. All joints are taped with joint compound leaving a thin coating of joint compound. Fastener heads are covered with a coat of joint compound. The finished surface should not have excess joint compound but some tool marks are okay. You might also see this finish in garages, storage or other areas where surface appearance is not that important.

Level 3 should only be used in areas that receive heavy texture before final painting or when a thick wall covering is applied. All joints are taped with joint compound. One additional coat of joint compound is applied over all joints. Fastener heads are covered with two separate coats of joint compound. All areas should be smooth and free of dust. The surface is prepared and covered with drywall primer prior to the application of the final finish.

Level 4 should be the standard residential grade for flat or satin paints. You should be careful using eggshell finish especially in areas that have raking light. All joints are taped with joint compound with two additional coats of joint compound. Fastener heads should be covered with three separate coats of joint compound. The surface must be smooth and free of dust. The surface is prepared and covered with a drywall primer. After the primer is applied any flaws in the surface should be repaired (point up*) and re-primed before the final finish.

Level 5 is the highest level of finish and is the most effective method to minimize the possibility of the tape or fasteners showing through the final finish. It is best used when semi gloss or gloss paint are used or where critical lighting conditions occur. All joints are taped with joint compound with two additional coats of joint compound. Fastener heads are covered with three coats of joint compound. A thin skim coat of joint compound is applied to the entire surface. The surface must be smooth and free of dust. The surface is prepared and covered with a drywall primer. After the primer is applied any flaws in the surface should be repaired (point up*) and re-primed before the final finish.

APPENDIX M

CONTRACTOR'S NAME AND ADDRESS

FINAL PUNCH LIST

Date_____ Job Number_____

Owner_____

Address_____

_____

I request the following items listed below be completed or corrected.

	ITEM		COMPLETED	
ROOM		DESCRIPTION	Owners Initials	Date

1. _____ |____|____|____|

2. _____ |____|____|____|

3. _____ |____|____|____|

4. _____ |____|____|____|

5. _____ |____|____|____|

6. _____ |____|____|____|

7. _____ |____|____|____|

8. _____ |____|____|____|

9. _____ |____|____|____|

10. _____ |____|____|____|

.

Owner_____ Date_____

Contractor_____ Date_____

APPENDIX N

LIEN WAIVER

On this date _____**CONSTRUCTION COMPANY NAME** has paid in full **NAME OF COMPANY WHO DID THE WORK** for all labor, services, equipment or material furnished to NAME OF CLIENT AND PROJECT ADDRESS. Therefore, **NAME OF COMPANY WHO DID THE WORK** does hereby waive and release any right to mechanic's lien or stop notice against NAME OF CLIENT(S)

CONSTRUCTION COMPANY NAME

By: _____
      AUTHORIZED REPRESENTATIVE

By: _____
      NAME OF COMPANY WHO DID THE WORK

GLOSSARY

ACAP: As Close As Possible.

Allowance: an allotted amount of money for a particular item, such as a toilet, light fixture, etc.

Alternate pricing (AP): a portion of the work that is priced separately and/or different priced products for a particular aspect of the construction. Giving the owner(s) a choice on defining the scope of the project.

Change order (CO): work that is added to or deleted from the original scope of work of a contract.

Concealment inspection (close-in): the Plumbing, Electrical and HVAC subcontractors have completed the first phase of their jobs. The plumbing pipes are run, sealed and secured; the bathtubs and shower pans are installed. The electrical cable is run and connected to the electrical panel, sub panel, all electrical boxes, and recessed lights. The HVAC unit is placed and all ductwork installed, sealed, secured, and insulated were applicable. The plumbing pipes are filled with air and an air pressure gauge is attached; the bathtubs and shower pans are filled with water. There is no insulation or drywall installed so everything including the framing can be inspected. The inspector also checks the framing to make sure that nothing structural has been compromised by the subcontractors.

Cross section: the vertical plane cut through the object. Sections describe the relationship between different levels of a building.

Detail: a small part of an aspect of construction at a larger scale showing how the component parts fit together. Usually showing complex junctions (such as floor to wall junction, complex eve junctions, and window openings) that cannot be clearly shown on a full drawing. They can also be used to show small surface details.

Devices: switches, outlets, surface mounted lights, and ceiling fans.

Durock: USG Brand Cement Board is moisture and mold resistant backer material for use under tile.

Electrical service panel: also known as a load center, service panel, breaker box or electrical panel, is a steel box that holds multiple circuit breakers wired to circuits that distribute power throughout your home.

Elevation: a flat view of a building seen from one side; each elevation is labeled in relation to the compass direction it faces.

Floor area ratio: gross (total) floor area to the square footage of the property (land). This could include non-covered areas too.

Floor Plan: a drawing showing a view from above of one level that is to scale with dimensions of all walls, rooms, and spaces.

FSC: The Forest Stewardship Council, an organization that sets standards for responsible forest management.

GC: General Contractor, the person responsible for oversight and management of a construction site, including vendors and trades; is the conduit for all communication of information to all involved parties throughout the entirety of a building project.

Fiber-Cement board: a building product offering weather and water resistant properties.

Finish Schedule: See Specification Sheet.

HVAC: Heating, Ventilation and Air Conditioning.

IBC: International Building Code, a model building code developed by the International Code Council (ICC). It has been adopted and use as a base code standard throughout most of the United States.

Lot coverage: the percentage of the lot area that is covered by building area, which includes the total horizontal area when viewed in plan. Jurisdictions might have different standards for what constitutes lot coverage.

LVLs: (Laminated Veneer Lumber) an engineered wood product that is used for long spans because of its superior tin strength to traditional dimensional lumber. The LVL is comprised of multiple thin layers of wood glued with adhesives.

MACAP: match as closely as possible.

OPCI: Owner Provided Contractor Installed.

Plumb: the upright surface is level such as the 2x4s of a wall.

Point-up: the application of joint compound and sanding of any defects in the drywall finish prior to applying the final finish coat.

PM: Project Manager, the person who is responsible for the planning, procurement and execution of the entire project. Project managers are first point of contact for any issues or discrepancies.

Roof Ridge: the highest point of the roof where two or more roof planes meet.

Rough-in: the plumbing electrical and HVAC subcontractors have completed the first phase of their jobs. The plumbing pipes are run, sealed and secured; the bathtubs and shower pans are installed. The electrical cable is run and connected to the electrical panel, sub panel, all electrical boxes, and recessed lights. There are no other devices installed. The HVAC unit is placed and all ductwork installed, sealed, secured, and insulated were applicable.

SBO: Supplied By Owner.

Scale: a ratio of relative size. A drawing in which one inch on paper represents one foot in reality would be expressed as 1:1.

Section: a view used on a drawing to show an area or hidden part of an object by cutting away and removing some of that object that blocks it.

Selection sheet: a comprehensive list of all of the selections for the construction project. It can include time frames for when your selection need to be finalized.

Set back: the distance that a building or other structure is set back from the property line (including the roof eaves). However, this could include areas that are within your property line but need protection such as body of waters or protected land.

Sheen: the paint's glossiness (flat, matte, satin, eggshell, semi-gloss, gloss).

Site plan: an architectural plan (landscape or building) drawing of proposed improvements to a given lot.

Specification sheet: might also be called "finish schedule", a detailed list of all of the material to be supplied and used on the construction project. This should be included in the contract documents.

Subfloor: the substrate material under the finished floor material.

Subpanel: an electrical panel that is feed from the main electrical panel to service a particular area of the house.

Subs: subcontractors. A person or persons hired by the general contractor to perform a specific job as part of the overall project such as plumbing, electrical, flooring, siding, roofing etc.

Sub walk: a group meeting on the proposed jobsite of all the major participants. These include the GC, framer, electrician, plumber, HVAC contractor and possibly the architect. It allows everyone involved to walk through the site with the actual architectural plans to better understand what their roles are. The scope and size of the project will determine who should be at this meeting.

Tankless Water Heater (TWH): does not store water like a traditional water tank. A TWH monitors the water flowing through the heating elements of the heater hence the term "on demand". The water is only heated when the hot water is turned on.

TBD: To Be Determined.

Value engineer: to look for substitutes for products and/or finishes to reduce the costs of construction. Sometimes this leads to better finish product too.

NOTES

NOTES

NOTES

NOTES

NOTES

NOTES

www.ingramcontent.com/pod-product-compliance
Lightning Source LLC
Chambersburg PA
CBHW081156290426

44108CB00018B/2575